AN INTRODUCTION TO
ROMAN HISTORY
LITERATURE
AND ANTIQUITIES

THE FOUNDATION OF ROME: AN ITALIAN HILL TOWN

Photograph by Mr. R. Gardner

A. PETRIE, M.A.

AN INTRODUCTION TO
ROMAN HISTORY
LITERATURE
AND
ANTIQUITIES

THIRD EDITION

GREENWOOD PRESS, PUBLISHERS
WESTPORT, CONNECTICUT

Library of Congress Cataloging in Publication Data

Petrie, Alexander.
    An introduction to Roman history, literature, and
antiquities.

    Reprint of the ed. published by Oxford University
Press, London.
    1. Rome--Civilization. I. Title.
[DG77.P45 1979]   937'.6   78-25840
ISBN 0-313-20848-4

Copyright Oxford University Press 1963.

First edition 1918
Second edition 1938
Third edition 1963

This reprint has been authorized by the Oxford University
Press.

Reprinted in 1979 by Greenwood Press, Inc.
51 Riverside Avenue, Westport, CT 06880

Printed in the United States of America

10 9 8 7 6 5 4 3 2 1

CONTENTS

LIST OF MAPS

AUTHOR'S NOTE

For the purpose of the third edition the whole text
has been revised by Mr. E. W. Gray, of Christ
Church, to whom the writer wishes to acknow-
ledge his obligations.

June 1963   A.P.

ROMAN HISTORY TO 23 B.C.

§ 1. The Latin Plain

The district which was the scene of Rome's early history was a narrow, low-lying strip of country enclosed between the Tiber and the Volscian highlands, and between the slopes of the Apennines and the sea. Towards the north-western extremity of this area, on the left bank of the Tiber and some fifteen miles above its mouth, a group of low hills must have marked from the first the natural site of a city which was to dominate the surrounding plain, and it was here that Rome was built.

§ 2. Early Rome: the Traditions

Roman tradition carried the story of the beginnings of the City even farther back than the arrival of Aeneas and his followers in Italy after the fall of Troy; but we may take up the thread at this point. Aeneas, so ran the tale, landed in Italy in the reign of King Lătīnus, whose people were called, after him, 'Latini' (perhaps = 'the people of the plain'). Aeneas married Latinus' daughter, Lavinia, and, on the death of the former, ruled over the united Trojans and Latins. Aeneas was succeeded by his son Ascanius (or Iulus), who founded Alba Longa, the seat of a line of Alban kings. In the reign of the last of these kings, Numitor, the twin brothers, *Rōmulus* and *Rĕmus*, were borne by the Vestal Rhea Silvia (daughter of Numitor) to the god Mars. Amulius, brother of Numitor, who had usurped the throne, ordered the children to be drowned in the Tiber, but they were miraculously preserved and suckled by a she-wolf. When the boys grew up, they slew the usurper and restored the throne to their grandfather. Soon after the brothers resolved to found a new city: the test of augury was resorted to, and the honour of founding and naming the city was awarded to Romulus, who established his town—Square Rome

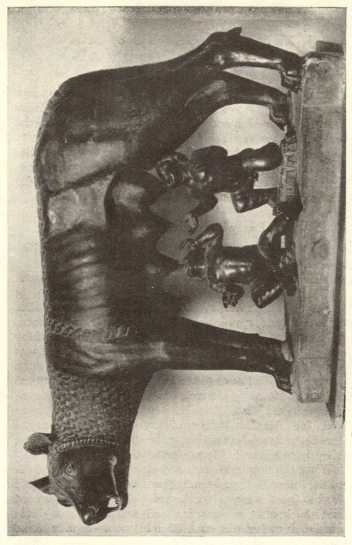

THE SHE-WOLF. Bronze, Museo Capitolino. The figures of Romulus and Remus were added during the Renaissance

(*Roma Quadrāta*)—on the Palatine hill, on 21 April 753 B.C. Remus was slain for leaping in scorn over his brother's wall.

§ 3. The Seven Kings of Rome

Continuing, the accepted tradition told of seven kings who ruled early Rome, with a more or less circumstantial account of their respective reigns:

(*a*) ROMULUS (753–717), in order to people his new city, opened an *asylum* or place of refuge for the blood-guilty and the exiled; fought with the Sabines, under their king Titus Tatius, and incorporated them with the Romans; and was finally caught up to heaven in a storm while reviewing his army in the Campus Martius.

(*b*) NUMA POMPILIUS (715–673), a Sabine, had a long and peaceful reign; instituted various priesthoods; and was regarded generally, at a later date, as the founder of the Roman state religion.

(*c*) TULLUS HOSTILIUS (673–642) made war upon and destroyed Alba Longa: with this struggle is connected the famous episode of the contest of the Horatii, three brothers born at a birth, on the Roman side, with a corresponding trio, the Curiatii, on the side of Alba. Forgetting, in his pride, the service of the gods, Tullus with his house was smitten by lightning from Jupiter.

(*d*) ANCUS MARCIUS (642–617) was a man of peace, as befitted the grandson of Numa, but had to conduct a war with the Latins. He built the first prison at Rome, fortified the hill Janiculum on the other side of the Tiber and connected it with the city by the *Pons Sublicius* (the pile-bridge), and founded a colony at Ostia at the mouth of the Tiber.

(*e*) LUCIUS TARQUINIUS PRISCUS (616–579), an Etruscan noble, was distinguished by great deeds both in peace and in war. He extended his sway widely over Latium; and among the notable public works which he carried out or planned were the building of a great temple to Jupiter on the Capitoline hill, the laying out of the *Circus Maximus* for races and games, and the construction of sewers (*clŏācae*) for draining the city. Politically, he increased the senate by a hundred new members, who were called *patres minorum gentium,* and doubled the number of the knights (*equites*).

(*f*) SERVIUS TULLIUS (578–535) continued the policy of his predecessor, especially in public works and internal reforms, but he also concluded an important alliance with the Latins. To Servius was due the great wall which enclosed the whole 'seven hills', and which long remained the legal limit of the City. Still more important and far-reaching was his organization of the people on a new basis of (primarily landed) property, instead of birth. The nature and significance of this reform will be noticed at another place.

(*g*) LUCIUS TARQUINIUS SUPERBUS (535–510), son of his predecessor of the same name, and son-in-law of Servius, exercised his rule with the same cruelty and violence by which he had compassed it. At home he oppressed the citizens; abroad he extended his power by war and marriage alliances, his most important conquest being the ancient Latin town of Gabii. He pushed on the public works which his father had begun, notably the Capitoline temple. But these works had imposed heavy burdens on the people, whose discontent became open revolt at the news of the outrage committed by Tarquin's son Sextus on a noble Roman matron, Lucretia. Tarquin was deposed and sentenced to exile with all his family. The kingly office was abolished, and in its place were substituted two annual magistrates called 'consuls' (*consules*),[1] who should exercise the supreme authority. The first consuls were Lucius Junius Brutus, nephew of Tarquin, who had headed the revolt, and Lucius Tarquinius Collatinus, the husband of Lucretia. Thus were the kings expelled, and Rome became a republic (509 B.C.).

§ 4. Fact and Fable: Who were the Romans?

The traditional account of the foundation, growth, and kings of early Rome must be largely discounted, because:

(*a*) The story crystallized centuries later than the events it

§ 3. [1] They were originally styled *praetores.*

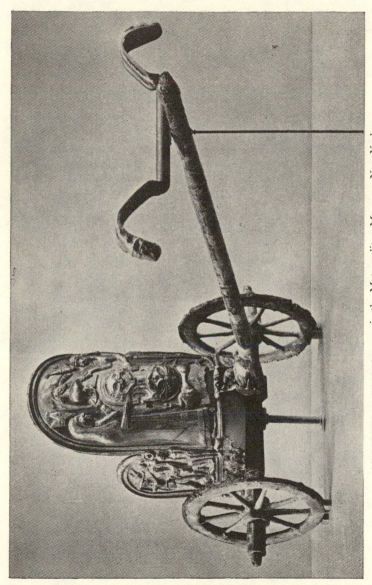

AN ETRUSCAN CHARIOT now in the Metropolitan Museum, New York

AN ETRUSCAN CHIEFTAIN AND HIS WIFE. Terra-cotta statues from their tomb at Cerveteri (Caere)
Villa Giulia, Rome, photograph Anderson

professes to record. Parts of it are a clumsy attempt to fill the gap between the fall of Troy (1184) and the foundation of Rome (753), and to combine native tradition with Greek speculation about Roman origins.

(*b*) Trustworthy records must have perished in the sack of Rome by the Gauls (390).

Despite these reservations, there is doubtless mingled with the traditions a certain amount of genuine historical fact. The following deductions may be regarded as established:

(*a*) That the Romans of history were one in blood with the Latin communities surrounding them, as their language and institutions show.

(*b*) That they contained an admixture of Sabine and Etruscan elements,[1] though these were comparatively unimportant.

(*c*) That the original nucleus of the city was on the Palatine hill.

(*d*) That the growth of the city consisted in the gradual fusion of separate communities, which process was probably complete by the reign of Servius Tullius.

(*e*) That in the latter part of the kingly period, Rome passed under the sway of powerful Etruscan princes—a conclusion supported by the traditional Etruscan origin of the Tarquins, the power of the Etruscans at this time, and the splendid public works with which the last three kings are credited.

(*f*) That, as in many Greek cities, monarchy gave way to oligarchy towards the close of the sixth century B.C., the kingship in Rome being replaced by a dual magistracy. Etruscan domination in Campania and Latium was crumbling at this time.

§ 5. The Roman Constitution under the Kings

The *Populus Romanus* or 'body politic' was divided into the three traditional tribes—*Ramnes*, *Tities*, and *Luceres*—names which may, or may not, point to ethnic distinctions.[1] More important

---

§ 4. [1] The names of the three original tribes—*Ramnes, Tities, Luceres*—are usually adduced as evidence in this connexion. But some theories make all three names Etruscan.   § 5. [1] See previous note.

was the division into thirty *curiae* or 'wards' based primarily on kinship and forming in turn the basis of religious, military, and political organization. The further division of each *curia* into a definite number of *gentes* ('clans') and 'families' cannot be maintained. All citizens, not simply the patricians, were members of the *curiae*.

(i) At the head of the state stands the king (*rex*), who is neither strictly hereditary nor strictly elective, and who is the supreme general, judge, and priest of the people.

(ii) The king is assisted by a senate or 'council of elders', originally of one hundred and afterwards of three hundred members.[2] These were the *patres*, selected from the leading *gentes*. Their chief prerogative was the proposing of a new king to the assembly, and the vote of the assembly required to be ratified by their sanction (*patrum auctoritas*). Once the king is elected, their relation to him is one of subordination, and they can advise him only when he chooses to consult them.

(iii) The popular assembly is the meeting of the members of the *curiae* in the *comitia curiata*, where the voting takes place *curiatim*, i.e. 'by wards'. The chief prerogative of the assembly was the acceptance or rejection of the king proposed to them by the *interrex* or representative of the *patres*. On other occasions they met merely to hear announcements by the king, who might also, of special grace, allow them to act as a court of appeal (*provocatio*) on a capital charge.

§ 6. Patricians, Clients, Plebeians

In Roman society the *gens* or 'clan' was of central importance, and within each *gens* the *familiae* ('households'), each presided over by its *paterfamilias*. Each *gens* had its own *sacra* (religious observances) and attached to it were *clientes* (dependants, lit. 'listeners'), who shared in the *sacra* and some of the other privileges of the full members, their *patroni* ('protectors'). An old and sharply marked distinction at Rome was that between *Patrician* and *Plebeian*. It is unlikely that the plebeians were

---

[2] See § 3 (*e*), above.

basically of different racial origin or that the patricians were the original settlers and the plebeians their clients or dependants. The fact that the plebeians were citizens was never in dispute. Class differences more probably arose gradually as a result of economic conditions. The plebeians had their own *gentes* and *sacra*. If the ban on intermarriage was first imposed only in 450 B.C., the emergence of a sharp distinction between the two orders must have been comparatively late. The *plebs* ('multitude') could have comprised clients whose patrons had become extinct as well as foreign settlers or members of conquered communities removed to Rome. Whatever their origin, the plebeians were certainly regarded by the patricians as incapable of sharing in their *sacra*, and this religious barrier was made to hedge round the privileges of the patricians in every direction.

§ 7. Reforms of Servius Tullius: the Comitia Centuriata

To appreciate the significance of the reforms of Servius, it must be remembered that the three tribes were also the basis of the original Roman army, which consisted of a legion of 3,000 infantry and 300 cavalry, one-third being furnished by each tribe. The Etruscan princes who ruled Rome had to find means of increasing their army for their foreign conquests. Tarquinius Priscus is credited with the intention of creating three new tribes and three new centuries of horsemen, but owing to opposition to his scheme, he achieved his purpose by doubling the strength of each division while leaving the existing forms unchanged.[1] A much more thoroughgoing reform is ascribed to Servius Tullius, who divided the whole people into four tribes —a *local* as opposed to a *birth* division[2]—the members of which were assessed (*censi*) according to the value of their property. There were constituted five property-divisions (*classes*), the richest of which formed the first line of infantry and also served

§ 7.   [1] The reforms of T. may have been confined to the cavalry.
  [2] This was important. The creation of new tribes made possible the incorporation of new elements in the citizen body, on the basis of domicile.

as cavalry,[3] the remaining classes serving as infantry less elaborately equipped in proportion to their rating. Each *classis*

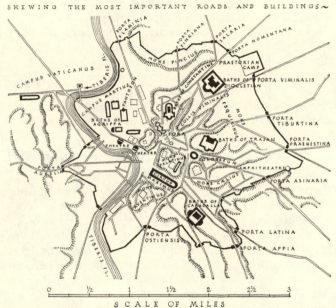

THE CITY OF ROME

IN THE TIME OF THE EMPERORS

SHEWING THE MOST IMPORTANT ROADS AND BUILDINGS

SCALE OF MILES

was divided into so many *centuriae* or units of no definite number,[4] to provide an equal number of centuries of *iuniores* (men below 46) and *seniores* (46 and above). The unclassified members, i.e. those whose property did not reach the standard of the fifth class, were *prōlētarii*.[5]

[3] The existing six centuries of cavalry were increased by other twelve drawn from the richest class.

[4] The number of individuals in the *centuriae* must have varied in the different *classes*.

[5] i.e. 'those who served the state only with their children' (*proles*).

The new arrangement, which extended to every citizen—patrician and plebeian alike—the privilege of serving in the army in a rank proportionate to his wealth, was unmistakably military in its aim;[6] but it is important to observe that it soon became a political organization, in which the *centuria* replaced the *curia* as the voting unit, and which gradually appropriated to itself all the more important functions of the *comitia curiata*.

§ 8. Disabilities of the Plebeians: Struggle between the Orders

The distinction between patrician and plebeian which has been already mentioned,[1] and the manner in which it operated, constitute the main interest of the internal history of Rome for more than two centuries after the foundation of the Republic. The plebeians had indeed gained something by the Servian reforms—the right of serving in the army and of voting in the new *comitia centuriata*; but their influence there must have been largely discounted by the predominance assigned to the wealthiest class,[2] by the fact that the proceedings were controlled by the consuls, who were patrician magistrates, and by the hampering effect of patrician sanction (*patrum auctoritas*)[3] in respect of both legislation and elections. But in addition to this, the *plebs* had other more specific grievances, e.g.:

(*a*) They were exposed to the despotic authority of the patrician consuls, against which there was no appeal;

(*b*) Of the public rights (*publica iura*) of the full citizen, they had not the *ius honōrum* or right of holding public office;

(*c*) Of the private rights (*privata iura*) they had not the *ius cōnūbii* or right of intermarriage with patricians;

(*d*) The law of debtor and creditor, which was very severe,

---

[6] The *comitia centuriata* which grew out of it was actually spoken of as *exercitus*.   § 8.   [1] § 6.

[2] The centuries of the first class and of the *equites* together amounted to more than half the total number.

[3] This expression is to be understood here as a vote of the whole (purely patrician) senate; after plebeians were admitted to seats in the senate, the *patres* most probably represent *the patrician section of the senate*.

bore hard on the plebeians, many of whom were poor. This was aggravated by the fact that the *ager publicus*, or state land, which had been won in war, was regarded as a patrician preserve;

(*e*) The patricians claimed to be the only true depositaries of the state law and religion, from the administration of which the plebeians were jealously excluded.

All these barriers were gradually broken down by the plebeians: we may notice the main tactics adopted by the respective sides in the long struggle:

(*a*) The plebeians, conscious of their importance in the army, take advantage of a military crisis to press a reform;

(*b*) The patricians fight them with all the weapons of evasion: particularly, when a magistracy is threatened, they diminish its importance by transferring some of its powers to a new official, *who must be a patrician*.

§ 9. Landmarks in the Struggle between the Orders

(*a*) The plebeians obtained protection against arbitrary treatment at the hands of patrician magistrates by

(i) The famous *Lex Valeria de provocatione* (509), allowing the right of appeal to the assembly of the centuries against a capital sentence passed by any magistrate;[1]

(ii) The appointment of two[2] officers of their own order (*tribuni plebis*), who were specially intended to protect them against the violence of the consuls,[3] and whose persons were to be inviolate (*sacrosancti*). This important concession, according to the traditional story, followed the *First Secession* of the plebs to the Sacred Mount[4] (*Mons Sacer*), 494 B.C.

(*b*) Several important bodies of legislation gradually won recognition for the plebs as a substantive elective and legislative body. These were, if we follow the tradition:

(i) The *Lex Publilia* (*Voleronis*) (471), by which the plebeians

§ 9. [1] Excepting a dictator.
[2] Probably: the number was afterwards raised to ten.
[3] They were said to have the *ius auxilii*.
[4] Across the Anio, about three miles from Rome.

obtained an assembly of their own (*concilium plebis*), with the right of electing their own officers and passing resolutions (*plebiscīta*).

(ii) The *Leges Valeriae Horatiae* (449), which gave *plebiscita*, under certain conditions, the force of laws.

(iii) The *Leges Publiliae* (339), which enacted that, in the case of measures proposed in the *comitia centuriata*, the *patrum auctoritas*[5] should be given beforehand.

(iv) The famous *Lex Hortensia* (287), which finally exempted *plebiscita* also (i.e. resolutions of the *concilium plebis*) from the *patrum auctoritas*, and made them valid and binding without reference to any other authority.

(*c*) The question of the *ager publicus*, first formally raised by an agrarian law of *Spurius Cassius* (486), was dealt with more thoroughly by the *Leges Liciniae Sextiae* (367), which restricted the amount of state land which a single citizen might occupy.

(*d*) An agitation raised by a tribune, *C. Terentilius Harsa* (462), with a view to limiting the powers of the consuls, resulted in the appointment of a body of ten[6] (*Decemviri*), who drew up the famous code of law (451), which, with a supplement added by a second board (450), became known as the 'TWELVE TABLES' (*Duodecim Tabulae*).[7]

(*e*) In the sphere of religion, the *Leges Liciniae Sextiae* (367) provided that half the college of keepers of the Sibylline books[8] should consist of plebeians, while the *Lex Ogulnia* (300) admitted plebeians even to the colleges of the augurs and pontiffs.[9]

(*f*) The *Lex Canuleia* (445) recognized *conubium* between the two orders.

(*g*) Concurrently with the above concessions, there was a steady advance in the throwing open to plebeians of state offices, on which some of the bodies of legislation above mentioned had a bearing.

---

[5] See § 8, n. 3.
[6] All patricians.
[7] The 'Tables' seem largely to have reaffirmed existing usages: the publication of them was the important thing.
[8] These were consulted in grave public crises.　　　　[9] § 90.

The proposal that a plebeian should be elected to the consulship (445) was evaded by a compromise providing that, instead of consuls, six 'military tribunes with consular power' (*tribuni militares consulari potestate*) should be elected, the new office to be open, theoretically,[10] to both orders alike. About the same time (443), the threatened loss of the consulship was provided for, to some extent, by the institution of a new patrician office—the censorship. But the *Leges Liciniae Sextiae*[11] (367) provided that in future consuls, and not military tribunes, should be elected, and that one of the consuls must be a plebeian; while the *Leges Publiliae* (339) enacted that one of the censors must be a plebeian.[12] With the guaranteed admission of plebeians to these two offices, practically the last stronghold of patrician privilege had been stormed: we may here append the dates of the opening of the various offices to the plebs:

First Plebeian Quaestor[13]			409 B.C.
,,	,,	Military Tribune	400
,,	,,	Consul	367
,,	,,	Dictator	356
,,	,,	Censor	351
,,	,,	Praetor	337

The long 'struggle between the orders' had thus ended in the plebeians securing complete social and political emancipation. Rome, at peace within herself, was now in a better position to complete the process of extending her dominion in Italy, which, in spite of the hampering effect of domestic quarrels, had been going steadily forward.

§ 10. The Roman Conquest of Italy

Only twelve years after the passing of the *Lex Hortensia*,[1] Rome had made herself mistress of the great bulk of the Italian

[10] No plebeians were actually elected until 400 B.C., but the plebeian pressure is shown by the fact that military tribunes instead of consuls were chosen in fifty out of the seventy-eight years, 444–366 B.C.

[11] Proposed 376, passed 367.

[12] A plebeian had been censor for the first time in 351.

[13] Plebeians had been eligible in theory as early as 421.

§ 10. [1] § 9 (*b*) (iv).

peninsula between the Po and the Straits of Messina. We may distinguish successive stages in this advance.

First Period: 509–450 B.C.

Under the Tarquins, Rome had extended her sway southwards over Latium and into southern Etruria on the north, and was already marked out as the champion of the plain country against the peoples of the mountainous regions surrounding it —Sabines, Aequians, and Volscians.[2] With the expulsion of the kings comes a marked shrinkage of power, and the resources of the infant republic are sorely taxed in a struggle for existence against enemies on every side.

(a) The Tarquins, in an attempt to recover their lost power, enlisted the aid first of *Lars Porsĕna*,[3] prince of the Etruscan town of Clusium, and then of the Latins under *Octavius Mamilius* of Tusculum. The Latins were defeated in a bloody battle at *Lake Regillus* (c. 497).

(b) The Sabines, Aequians, and Volscians carried their raids up to the very gates of Rome, while to the north of the Tiber Rome had a dangerous neighbour in the powerful Etruscan city of *Veii*. Threatened by so many foes, Rome concluded a most useful and very natural treaty with the Latin communities[4] (493): the alliance of the *Hernĭci* followed some years later (c. 486). In 474 some relief was obtained by a forty years' peace with Veii, but despite this advantage, the period is one of weakness.

Second Period: 450–390 B.C.

The second period is distinctly more favourable to Rome. In southern Etruria the capture of Veii (396) was an important success, and not many years later 'Latin' colonies were planted at *Sutrium* and *Nĕpĕte*.[5] The Sabines are quiescent; the Aequi

---

[2] The sections dealing with external history should be followed with a good map.

[3] Also spelt *Porsenna*. With the invasion of Porsena is connected the famous story of Horatius Cocles.   [4] Treaty of Sp. Cassius.

[5] Important positions in southern Etruria.

appear before the gates of Rome for the last time in 446, and the strength of the Volsci is broken by repeated attacks. Rome's progress is facilitated by the decline of Etruria.

Third Period: 390–343 B.C.

At the beginning of this period, Rome's very existence was threatened by the sack of the city by the Gauls, a branch of the Celtic race, in the course of one of their periodical inundations of southern Europe. The Romans were defeated in a disastrous battle on the *Allia*[6] (390), some miles from the city: Rome became the spoil of the invaders, but the Capitol remained intact. After besieging it for seven months, the Gauls suddenly disappeared, probably for reasons other than those given by Roman historians, and Rome quickly recovered from the visitation. Her hold on southern Etruria was maintained by the planting of colonies and the creation of four new local tribes in this district: *Caere*, which submitted in 353, was a little later incorporated with the Roman state as the first *civitas sine suffragio*.[7]

The Aequi and Volsci were still further weakened: *Antium*, formerly Latin, but at this time a centre of Volscian resistance to Rome, was deprived of part of its territory in 358.[8] It finally became a Roman colony in 338. In the meantime, Rome was called upon to deal with some disaffected Latin cities—members of the Latin league—which were probably beginning to view with apprehension the growing power of Rome. *Tusculum* was incorporated with the Roman state and received the full franchise. The old alliance with the Latins and Hernĭci was renewed in 358, presumably on less favourable terms. On the whole, the period is one of marked advance on the part of Rome, who adds considerably to her territory north and south.

---

[6] A tributary of the Tiber on its left bank.

[7] i.e. a community which enjoyed the rights of Roman citizenship without the privilege of voting in the Roman assemblies. Hence the phrase *Caeritum tabulae* applied to a limited franchise of this kind.

[8] Two new tribes, Pomptina and Publilia, were formed in this district.

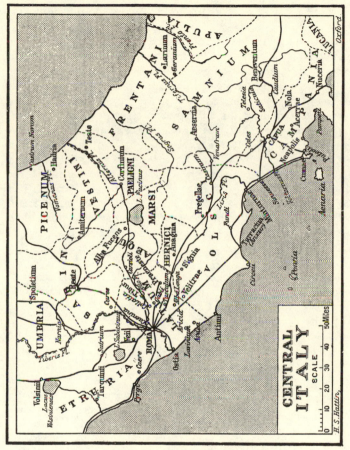

ROME AND HER NEIGHBOURHOOD

Fourth Period, 343–290 B.C.: Samnite and Latin Wars

As the acknowledged champion of the low countries against their neighbours of the surrounding highlands, Rome was next invited to assist the people of Campania[9] against a formidable enemy, the *Samnites*—an offshoot of the Umbro-Sabellian tribes that had rapidly spread over central and southern Italy. Thus began the *First Samnite War* (343), which after two indecisive campaigns was ended by a treaty (341), and Rome was fortunate in gaining time for a greater struggle which involved her very existence. This was the effort of her Latin allies to overthrow the position of Rome as the now dominant city in the Latin league. In a pitched battle at *Trifanum* the Romans, allied with the Samnites, broke the back of the Latin resistance, and Rome at once proceeded to consolidate her dominion in Latium. The old Latin league was dissolved, and five[10] at least of the Latin cities were compelled to accept the Roman franchise. The rest, with the Latin colonies, were organized on a basis of isolation from one another and of closer dependence upon Rome.

The real struggle between Rome and Samnium was still to come. The Capuan request to Rome to eject a Samnite garrison from Neapolis in Campania and the alliance of Rome with the liberated city led to the outbreak of the *Second Samnite War*, which lasted twenty-three years (327–304). The early years of the campaign were marked by the memorable reverse to the Roman arms at the CAUDINE FORKS (*Furculae Caudīnae*), where the Roman army under the two consuls of the year, T. Veturius and Sp. Postumius, was trapped in a narrow defile and compelled to surrender (321), the terms of capitulation being afterwards repudiated by the senate. Half-way through the campaign, however, the tide began to turn: Rome had been fortunate in isolating Apulia and Lucania from the Samnite cause, while she surrounded Samnium at the same

---

[9] The Campanians themselves were Sabellians, but they in course of time had lost all sense of community with the Samnites who now attacked them.

[10] Lanuvium, Aricia, Nomentum, Pedum, Tusculum.

time with a chain of fortresses, and built the *Via Appia*[11] to secure her communications with Campania. In 305 a Samnite army was defeated and their allies put out of action. Peace was concluded the following year (304), the Samnites being granted honourable terms which respected at least their local independence.

The next few years were spent by Rome in steadily confirming her conquests in central Italy. Already, before the conclusion of the Samnite War, her old allies, the Hernici, who

ROCCA DI PAPA (MONS ALBANUS) FROM TUSCULUM
Photograph by Mr. R. Gardner

had revolted, had been compelled to enter the Roman state as *cives sine suffragio,* and about the same time the Aequi, her old enemies, finally submitted. Several of the Sabellian tribes between Latium and the Adriatic seaboard became her allies. In northern Etruria she had made her power felt by defeating the Etruscans at *Lake Vadimo* (310). Twelve years after the battle at Lake Vadimo, a coalition of Samnites, Etruscans, Umbrians, and Gauls made a last desperate effort to break the supremacy of Rome which is known as the *Third Samnite War* (298–290). A decisive Roman victory at *Sentinum* (295) in

[11] So called after Appius Claudius Caecus the Censor.

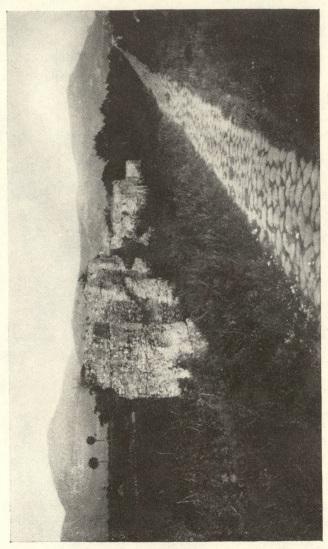

PAVING OF AN ANCIENT ROMAN ROAD. The Via Appia, and tombs by its side

Photograph by Mr. R. Gardner

Umbria broke the strength of this confederation, but the Samnites continued the struggle single-handed for some years longer till 290, when they were finally reduced by *M'. Curius Dentatus* and admitted to alliance with Rome on equal terms.

Summing up the results of this long period of conflict, we may say that Rome—

(*a*) Secures her hold on Latium and Campania.

(*b*) Protects her conquests by a chain of colonies.

(*c*) Extends her influence, by means of alliances, into all parts of Italy.

(*d*) Appears as the champion of Italy against the Gauls.

Fifth Period, 290–264 B.C.: *The War with Pyrrhus*

In the interval between the conclusion of the Third Samnite War and the landing of Pyrrhus in Italy, Rome found means, as usual, to consolidate her position in central Italy by the planting of colonies and the annexation of the Sabine territory, while farther north she conducted successful campaigns against the Celtic Sěnŏnes and Boii (284–282), which secured comparative peace to northern Italy for more than a generation. But the next serious trouble was to come from the opposite extremity of the peninsula. The Sabellian tribes, being gradually forced southward, had begun to harass the Greek cities of the southern seaboard, who invoked the aid of Rome in consideration of their recognizing Roman suzerainty. The appeal was listened to, and several of the cities were occupied by Roman garrisons; but the powerful city of *Tarentum* determined to make a stand for independence, and found a champion in *Pyrrhus*, king of Epirus, a Greek soldier of fortune, who seems to have cherished ideas of a great empire in the West. In the first two battles of the campaign—at *Heraclēa* (280) and *Ascŭlum* (279)—victory declared for Pyrrhus, largely owing to his elephants; but the Roman strength was unbroken, and Pyrrhus, impatient, crossed over to Sicily, where he won a series of victories over the Carthaginians. Returning to Italy in 276, he found the

Romans gaining ground and his allies deserting him in disgust. In the following year (275), the battle of *Beneventum*, which ended in a complete victory for the Romans, closed Pyrrhus' career in Italy. He returned to Greece, leaving Rome free to crush out the last efforts of his allies at resistance. Tarentum surrendered in 272, and, with other cities, was added to the Roman allies. A number of colonies,[12] in true Roman fashion, were established in Samnium and Lucania, while the Adriatic coast was similarly strengthened.

§ 11. Extent and Organization of 'Italy' at the close of the War with Pyrrhus

The war with Pyrrhus left Rome mistress of 'Italy', by which term is to be understood roughly the part of the peninsula south of a line drawn from Pisa to Ancona. Beyond this limit lay Ligurians and Gauls, who were to be incorporated at a later date.

Within this area, the Roman state proper comprised, territorially, (*a*) on the west, the greater part of southern Etruria, Latium, and Campania, (*b*) in the centre, the former territories of the Aequi, Hernici, and Sabines, (*c*) on the east, part, at least, of Picenum; and was represented by a citizen body of some 300,000, who may be distinguished as:

(*a*) CIVES ROMANI or full Roman citizens, consisting of (i) members of the thirty-three[1] tribes into which the Roman territory was divided, (ii) members of *Coloniae Romanae* (Roman colonies), which were planted to guard different parts of Italy, especially the coasts of Latium and Campania, (iii) members of communities which had received the full Roman franchise.[2]

(*b*) MUNICIPIA or communities which had received the partial Roman franchise (*civitas sine suffragio*), e.g. Caere.[3]

---

[12] Paestum, Beneventum, Aesernia.

§ 11. [1] The final number, thirty-five, was completed in 241.

[2] e.g. the five old Latin towns mentioned in § 10, n. 10.

[3] The term *municipium* was sometimes, however, applied loosely to any Roman town other than Rome itself.

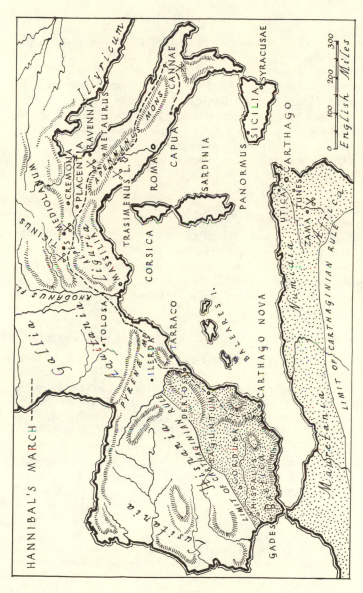

THE WESTERN MEDITERRANEAN IN THE TIME OF HANNIBAL

(*c*) Socii or allies, who were either (i) *Nomen Latinum* or (ii) *Socii* proper.

(i) The *Nomen Latinum* was the designation of a class of allies with special privileges, which generally included rights of trade and intermarriage with Rome.[4]

(ii) The *Socii* had their relation to Rome variously determined by the nature of their treaty (*foedus*), but, generally speaking, while they were independent in their internal affairs, their foreign relations were determined by Rome, and they provided contingents for service in the Roman armies.

As a rule, we can detect in Rome's treatment of her subjects the policy of (*a*) isolating them from one another, (*b*) attaching them closely to herself, (*c*) leaving them a certain amount of self-government and judicial autonomy, while (*d*) controlling the direction of their foreign affairs. Rome's generosity in extending varying degrees of citizenship to allied or conquered peoples was the underlying cause of her rise to predominance and of the durability and strength of the unique federation she created in Italy.

§ 12. Rome and the West: the Struggle with Carthage

So far Rome had not made her power felt outside of Italy although, since the beginning of the Republic, she had had intermittent commercial and political relations (embodied in a series of treaties) with the great Phoenician city of *Carthage*, which at this time controlled the trade of the western Mediterranean and had secured a firm footing in the islands of Sardinia and Sicily. Now she was drawn into a conflict with Carthage. The immediate occasion was the seizing of the Sicilian town of *Messāna* by a body of Campanian mercenaries, the *Māmertīni* ('Children of Mars'), who found themselves hard pressed by *Hiero*, king of Syracuse. In this plight, they resolved to apply to Rome for help. Rome, though in a difficult position owing to

---

[4] The 'Latin colonies' which enjoyed these rights were sent out originally by Rome and the other members of the old Latin league jointly; afterwards, when the league was dissolved, by Rome alone, but the style and privileges of the colonists remained with little change.

her being on friendly terms with Hiero, responded to the appeal and occupied Messana, which Hiero and the Carthaginians then besieged. Thus began the *First Punic War* (264–241).

A WAR-ELEPHANT carrying a tower full of armed men. An Italian plate recalling the invasion of Pyrrhus or Hannibal
Villa Giulia, Rome

Four periods may be distinguished in the struggle which followed:

(*a*) 264–261. The Romans (263) secure the valuable alliance of Hiero, who remains a firm friend, and in the next two years overrun the greater part of Sicily, capturing *Agrigentum* (262).

(b) 260–255. The Romans build their first fleet and win naval victories at *Mȳlae* (260), and *Ecnŏmus* (256), which open the way for the invasion of Africa. Here the consul *M. Atīlius Rēgulus*, after a series of victories, is disastrously defeated by the Carthaginians under *Xanthippus* and taken prisoner (255). The Roman fleet is wrecked on its way home with the survivors of Regulus' army.

(c) 254–249. After their failure in Africa the Romans prosecute the war in Sicily, and capture *Panormus*,[1] where they also win a great victory[2] some time after (251). These successes are counterbalanced by the loss of a second fleet in a storm (253), and the defeat of P. Claudius in a naval battle off *Drĕpăna*, in the west of Sicily (249).

(d) 248–241. The Romans, despairing of success by sea, concentrate their efforts on expelling the Carthaginians from Sicily; but *Hamilcar Barca*, the Carthaginian commander, defies all attempts to dislodge him from western Sicily, and the war languishes. The Romans at length determine on a final effort by sea, equip a new fleet, and gain a signal victory at the *Aegātes insulae* under *Lutatius Catulus* (242). Peace was concluded the following year (241) on condition that the Carthaginians should (a) evacuate Sicily, (b) restore Roman prisoners, (c) pay a heavy war indemnity. Among the main results of the war, (a) the Carthaginians lose Sicily; (b) Rome acquires her first province; (c) proves her strength as a sea-power.

§ 13. Events between the First and Second Punic Wars

In the interval between the First and Second Punic Wars, Rome was active in various directions, both inside and outside of Italy.

(a) Taking advantage of a mercenary war at Carthage, she seizes Corsica and Sardinia (238), which soon after are made a Roman province;

(b) Defeats the Gauls at *Tĕlămon* in Etruria (225); subdues the *Boii* and *Insŭbres* in the valley of the Po (by 222); and further

---

§ 12.   [1] Palermo.   [2] On land.

strengthens her hold on the north by the construction of the *Via Flaminia* to Arīmĭnum, and the foundation of 'Latin' colonies at *Placentia* and *Crĕmōna*.

(*c*) Chastises the Illyrian pirates on the opposite coast of the Adriatic, and sends envoys to Greece.

Carthage, on her part, employed the interval in building up a dominion in Spain under *Hamilcar* (236–228), *Hasdrubal* (228–221), and finally *Hannibal*, son of the first-named. A compact (*c.* 226) was arranged between Rome and Hasdrubal, recognizing the *Ibērus* (Ebro) as the northern limit of Carthaginian influence in Spain, and so leaving them a free hand south of that river, although Rome had earlier made an alliance with *Saguntum* in that region.

§ 14. The Second Punic War (218–201 B.C.)

Hannibal attacked and took Saguntum after a desperate resistance (219), in defiance of Roman protests. He broke no treaty in attacking Saguntum, but his deliberate action, which Carthage supported, was the immediate cause of the Second Punic War.

First Period: From Hannibal's Invasion of Italy to the Battle of Cannae (218–216)

Leaving *New Carthage* (Cartagena) early in 218, Hannibal crossed the Pyrenees, passed the Rhone, where the Romans had hoped to check him, crossed the Alps in spite of great difficulties and hardships and descended into Cis-Alpine Gaul. Here he defeated the Romans in battles on the *Tīcīnus* and *Trebia*, tributaries of the Po (218). Crossing the Apennines in the spring of next year (217), he annihilated *Flaminius* and his army at the *Trasimene Lake* (*Lacus Trăsŭmennus*). These successive defeats suggested the adoption of more cautious tactics on the Roman side, and for a time the policy of the dictator *Q. Fabius Maximus*—known as *Cunctator* or *the Lingerer*—at least averted disaster; but the popular discontent decreed that the Carthaginian should once again be faced in the open field. The result

A ROMAN WAR-ELEPHANT CARRYING A TOWER. Pompeii

was the crushing defeat of the consuls *Terentius Varro* and
Aemilius Paullus at *Cannae* (216), where the Romans were said to
have lost as many as 50,000 men. This victory was one more
proof of Hannibal's superiority in a pitched battle, and won
him new allies among the peoples of southern Italy; but the
Roman colonies, as a rule, stood firm, and the Roman spirit
was unbroken.

Second Period: From the Battle of Cannae to the Recovery of Capua
(216–211)

During the next five years the struggle ranged over a wide
area, partly through Hannibal's attempts to stir up enemies for
the Romans in other quarters.

(*a*) *Philip of Macedon* concluded a treaty with Hannibal, but
was unable to render any effective aid.

(*b*) In Sicily, Syracuse, now under Hiero's grandson, revolted,
and the main interest of the war centres there for the next two
years (214–212): the city was stormed by Marcellus in the
latter year.

(*c*) In Spain, the brothers Scipio, after a series of successes
against the Carthaginians, are defeated and killed, 211.

(*d*) In Italy, the most important event is the recovery (211)
of *Capua*, where Hannibal had wintered after his victory at
Cannae; but against this, Hannibal gained possession of *Taren-*
tum, though the Romans held the citadel.

General results: Hannibal's partial successes are insufficient
to divert the Romans from their main objective, the capture of
Capua, and he is forced more and more to the south. He
receives no material aid from outside sources. A great Roman
general is discovered in *P. Cornelius Scipio*, who afterwards completed the conquest of Spain.

Third Period: From the recovery of Capua to the end of the War
(211–201)

During this period Hannibal maintained a sullen defence in
the south of Italy, varied by occasional brilliant strokes;[1] but

§ 14. [1] Such as the ambushing and death of the consul Marcellus (208).

THE CIRCULAR HARBOUR AT OSTIA
Rome's port at the mouth of the Tiber
Photograph Chaundy

THE OUTER AND INNER HARBOURS OF ANCIENT CARTHAGE
from the air today
Photograph Ashmolean Museum

his hopes were now largely centred in the appearance in Italy of his brother *Hasdrubal*, who crossed the Alps to support him, but was defeated and slain at the river *Metaurus* (207), following on a daring march of the Roman consul *Nero* to join hands with his colleague *Livius*. The victory at the Metaurus practically decided the issue of the war in Italy, and about the same time Scipio had cleared Spain of the Carthaginians. Returning to Rome in 206, Scipio was elected consul for the following year, with permission to invade Africa. This he did in 204, and with the co-operation of *Masinissa*, a Numidian prince, won a number of successes, which led to Hannibal being recalled in order to oppose Scipio at home. Soon after, Scipio completely defeated Hannibal at *Zama* (202), and peace was declared the following year (201). Conditions: (*a*) Carthage to retain her independence and territory in Africa, but wage no wars without consent of Rome; (*b*) surrender all her ships, elephants, and prisoners of war; (*c*) pay an indemnity of 10,000 talents in fifty years.

§ 15. The Settlement of the West

Rome now stood forth as a great Mediterranean power, and had to face the task of setting in order the Carthaginian heritage on which she had entered. In so doing she laid the foundations of her great provincial system.

(i) SICILY, the earliest of her conquests, had already been defined as a province, and assigned to a praetor (227); another praetor was appointed at the same time to govern

(ii) SARDINIA, with CORSICA. The subsequent history of these islands under Roman rule was comparatively uneventful.

(iii) SPAIN was definitely organized as two provinces[1] in 197, and to govern these, two new praetors were appointed. The romanization of Spain was considerably thwarted by the war-like tribes of the interior, especially the *Celtiberians*. These were dealt with first by *M. Porcius Cato* (195) and then by *Ti. Sempronius Gracchus* (180–179), whose conciliatory policy was

§ 15. [1] Hispania Citerior and H. Ulterior, divided by the *Saltus Castulonensis*.

followed by thirty years of comparative tranquillity. After the insurrection of *Viriāthus* and the capture of *Numantia* by *Scipio Africanus the Younger* (133), the country was fairly peaceful, except for the *Astŭres* and *Cantabri* in the north-west, who were not finally subdued till the time of Augustus.

(iv) AFRICA. The territory of Carthage, whose integrity was nominally guaranteed by the treaty of 201, was in effect subject, probably with Roman connivance, to the encroachments of Masinissa, which the Carthaginians were finally obliged to resist by force of arms. This gave the anti-Carthaginian party in the Roman senate the handle they had long desired for removing the Carthaginian menace for all time. War (the *Third Punic War*) was declared in 150, and ended four years later with the capture and destruction of Carthage by *Scipio Africanus the Younger* (146). The territory of Carthage then became the Roman province of *Africa*, and the settlement of Carthage's former dominions under Roman sway was complete.

(v) GAUL. Though Gaul was not immediately affected by the struggle with Carthage, we may here glance at its fortunes in order to complete the survey of the West.

(a) *Cisalpine Gaul*. We have seen that Rome had secured a firm footing in the region immediately south of the Po between the First and Second Punic Wars (§13), and it will be a sufficient indication of the progress of romanization in this quarter from that time onward to state that the Transpadane communities received 'Latin rights' (*ius Latinum*) in 89,[2] when their southern neighbours received the full franchise, and that the whole of Cisalpine Gaul was formed into a province not many years after (*c.* 81 B.C.).

(b) *Transalpine Gaul*. Rome first had occasion to interfere here in order to protect her old and faithful ally, *Massīlia* (Marseilles), against the raids of the neighbouring Ligurian tribes (125). Victories followed over the *Allobrŏges* and *Arverni* (121) and Rome proceeded to consolidate her position by constituting as a *provincia* or 'sphere of influence' a vaguely defined district on

---

[2] By the *Lex Pompeia*. They were fully enfranchised by Caesar (49).

either side of the Rhone, extending roughly from the Maritime
Alps to the Pyrenees. This region was known either simply as
'Provincia' (*Provence*) or as 'Gallia Narbonensis', from the
colony of *Narbo Martius* founded for its protection (118).

§ 16. Rome and the East: Macedonian and Syrian Wars

At the time when Rome had occasion to interfere seriously in
the affairs of the East, the crumbling empire of Alexander the
Great was represented by three main powers:—(i) *Macedonia,*

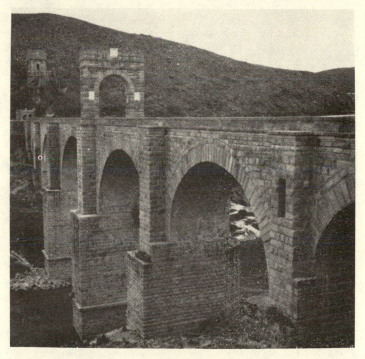

A ROMAN BRIDGE BUILT BY TRAJAN, crossing the Tagus, at Alcántara,
Spain
Photograph Beamish

under *Philip V*; (ii) *Syria*, under *Antiochus III*; (iii) *Egypt*, under *Ptolemy Philopator*. Of these, Egypt had long been in friendly alliance with Rome. Besides these larger powers, there were minor political combinations such as the *Aetolian* and *Achaean Leagues* in Greece, while the island state of Rhodes was of some importance as a naval power. Rhodes, and also *Attalus*, king of *Pergamum*, a new kingdom which had arisen in Mysia, had formed alliances with Rome for their protection.

§ 17. First and Second Macedonian Wars

The first collision came with Macedonia. We have seen how Philip, as early as 214 B.C., had menaced Rome by an alliance with Hannibal.[1] Rome, however, contrived to keep him busy at home by organizing against him a confederacy of anti-Macedonian states,[2] and a treaty concluded in 205, practically on the basis of the *status quo*, terminated the so-called *First Macedonian War*.

Shortly after, when Philip, taking advantage of the upset of the balance in the East caused by the death of Ptolemy Philopator, not only entered into an arrangement with Antiochus of Syria for the partition of the dominions of Egypt, but also attacked various Greek cities, the senate forced the reluctant *Comitia* to declare war on Macedon (*Second Macedonian War*). Philip's allies were not enthusiastic in his cause, and he was finally defeated at *Cynoscephălae*, in Thessaly, by *T. Quinctius Flaminīnus* (197). He was left undisturbed in his kingdom of Macedonia, but deprived of all outside possessions. The 'freedom of Greece' was proclaimed amid great enthusiasm at the Isthmian Games (196), and Rome, who as yet had no idea of acquiring fresh territory, withdrew her troops (194).

§ 18. The Syrian War

Antiochus, who had been unable to render his ally Philip any effective help on the European side of the Aegean, overran Asia

§ 17.   [1] § 14 (Second Period).
[2] Notably the Aetolian League, with which Rome formed an alliance.

Minor, and finally at the invitation of the Aetolians, who were dissatisfied with the results of Cynoscephalae, crossed into Greece. He was met and defeated by a Roman force under *M'. Acilius Glabrio* at the pass of *Thermopylae* (191), whereupon he withdrew again to Asia Minor. Here he was finally overthrown at *Magnēsia* in 190 by L. Scipio, who was accompanied by his brother Publius, the conqueror of Hannibal. Antiochus' sphere of influence was bounded by the Halys–Taurus line, which he was forbidden to cross, and Pergamum and Rhodes were strengthened by gifts of territory. In Asia, as in Macedonia, Rome was content for the time being with the establishment of a protectorate as against a policy of annexation. But her hand was soon forced in the latter direction.

§ 19. Third Macedonian War

Philip as Rome's ally had aided her in the war with Antiochus, but his position was aggravated, if anything, by the peace of Magnesia, and until his death in 179 B.C. he laboured quietly to strengthen it. His work was continued by his son and successor, *Perseus*, who, partly through the intrigues of King Eumenes of Pergamum, failed to allay Roman suspicions. War came in 171, and Perseus, after some initial success, was totally defeated by the consul *Lucius Aemilius Paullus* in a great battle at *Pydna* (168). Perseus was brought a prisoner to Rome, and died shortly after.

§ 20. Settlement of the East: New Roman Provinces

Even after Pydna Rome still hesitated to apply the provincial system in its entirety to the kingdom of Perseus; but the attempt of the pretender *Andriscus* to resuscitate the monarchy brought matters to a head, and *Macedonia* became a regular province under a Roman governor (146).

In Greece, several years of mutual jealousies and bickerings between rival factions culminated in a war with the *Achaeans*, who were easily defeated, and *Corinth* was taken and destroyed by *L. Mummius* in 146, the same year which witnessed the

destruction of Carthage.[1] As a result, the whole country up to
the borders of Macedonia and Epirus was placed under the
control of the governor of Macedonia, with which it formed
the province of *Macedonia and Achaia* (145).

In Asia Minor, an even looser control than Rome had
originally exercised over Macedonia and Greece was attended
with somewhat similar results. Rhodes and Pergamum, her
faithful allies, gradually declined in power, partly through the
neglect and partly with the connivance of Rome, and this
tended to increase the general disorder. Finally, on the death of
Attalus III, the last king of Pergamum, who bequeathed his
dominions to Rome, part of them became the Roman province
of *Asia* (133).

Rome was now supreme in both the eastern and the western
Mediterranean, but the progress of romanization was not alike
in both. In the West it was rapid, because there was no previous
deep-rooted civilization to replace, but in the East Rome made
no attempt to romanize the Greeks, and Greek civilization
and the Greek language maintained their ground. It was the
policy of Rome not to interfere unduly with the existing order
of things.

§ 21. Roman Provincial Administration

The extension of Rome's dominion overseas necessitated the
invention of machinery for organizing her conquests. The term
provincia signified originally the 'sphere of action' of a magistrate
with *imperium*, and the transition was easy to the district over
which such *imperium* was exercised. Each province was organized under a charter (*lex provinciae*), which was usually prepared
by the general who had conquered the country,[1] assisted by a
commission appointed by the senate. This charter determined
the limits of the province, the number and status of the communities included in it, the method and amount of the taxation
(*vectīgal, stīpendium*), along with other particulars; but in many
matters outside the charter the governor for the time being

§ 20.   [1] § 15 (iv).
§ 21.   [1] Thus we have the *Lex Rupilia* (Sicily), *Lex Pompeia* (Bithynia), &c.

possessed dangerously wide powers of discretion. Originally the government of a province was entrusted to one of the praetors, but as provinces were multiplied the practice was adopted of creating special 'pro-magistrates', who were invested with the imperium *pro consule* or *pro praetore*.[2] The governor was accompanied from Rome by a quaestor as his financial agent, a number of *lēgāti* or 'deputy-governors', a staff of personal friends (*cohors*), and other officials.

The complete list of the provinces under the republic, with the dates of their organization, may here be given:—Sicily,[3] 241; Sardinia (with Corsica),[4] 231; the two Spains,[5] 197; Macedonia and Achaia, 146–145; Africa, 146; Asia, 133; Gallia Narbonensis[6] (Provincia), 120; Gallia Cisalpina, *c.* 81; Bithynia (74) and Pontus (65); Crete (67) and Cyrene[7] (74); Cilicia (originally constituted 102, reorganized 64) and Cyprus, 58; Syria, 64.

§ 22. Internal Changes at Rome during the Great Wars

Up to the point which we have reached, the energies of Rome had been almost wholly absorbed in her foreign conquests; and though she was destined to add still further to her dominions, East and West, it is true to say that from this point onwards the main interest of Roman history changes from external conquest to problems affecting Rome and Italy, which gradually resolve themselves into the problem of what the future government of Rome is to be. While the great wars were in progress, certain changes had come over the Roman state and Roman society, and these changes were intimately connected with the

[2] The republican practice was to appoint a 'proconsul' to a province where a military force was required, a 'propraetor' to one which was peaceful.

[3] Western portion ceded by Carthaginians.

[4] Two new praetors for the government of this and Sicily were appointed in 227.   [5] i.e. Hispania Citerior and Ulterior.

[6] Caesar's conquests 58–50 B.C. added the rest of the country as far as the Rhine.

[7] The two were not always conjoined: the same applies to Cilicia and Cyprus.

constitutional struggle which began with the Gracchi and which was to end only with the establishment of the empire. We may consider these changes under the heads of—A. Political, B. Social, and C. Economic.

A. POLITICAL. (i) An outstanding fact at the close of the great wars was the enormously enlarged scope of the powers of the

A ROMAN SESTERTIUS OF THE FIRST CENTURY A.D.
The letters S C (senatus consulto) are the mark of the senate without whose authority no bronze coin could be issued.
Photograph Chaundy

senate, which controlled practically at will both the internal and the foreign policy of the Roman state. While strictly subordinate in theory to the magistrates and the great public assemblies, the senate had, for various reasons, acquired a predominant position at the expense of both.

(*a*) The system of yearly magistrates did not make for consistency in foreign policy, the control of which naturally passed to a strong, permanent, central authority, on which the magistrates more and more tended to lean.

(*b*) The senate, being largely composed of ex-magistrates, might be said to represent the concentrated political experience of the state.

(c) It was convened much more easily than the *comitia*, many of the members of which lived at a great distance from Rome, and which were too often represented only by the incompetent city crowd.

The weakness of the senate's position was that these enlarged powers did not rest on any sound constitutional basis; nevertheless it was not prepared to surrender them without a struggle when the challenge came.

(ii) A *new nobility* had grown up, represented by those plebeian families which had attained to curule[1] office since the admission of plebeians to the magistracies, and which did their best to keep such offices in their own hands to the exclusion of the *novus homo*.[2]

B. SOCIAL. The opening up of the eastern world to Rome, and the influx of wealth which accompanied it, exercised an injurious influence on the old Roman character as embodied e.g. in Cato the Censor, who vainly strove against the decadent tendencies of his day.

C. ECONOMIC. In earlier days the Roman soldier after a campaign returned to cultivate his farm: this was no longer possible when wars were waged overseas and the troops were absent for a prolonged period. Moreover, the importation of corn from abroad made its production in Italy less profitable. The direct results of this were the decay of the yeoman-farmer class and the accumulation of estates in the hands of the wealthy, who employed large gangs of slaves.

§ 23. The Gracchi head an Attack on the Senate

It was in connexion with the economic question that the authority of the senate was first to be assailed. *Tiberius Gracchus* as tribune (133 B.C.) introduced a scheme of land reform which provided for the allotment among the poorer citizens of so much of the state lands as was not held by duly authorized

---

§ 22. [1] § 54.

[2] A Roman who, like Cicero, was the first of his family to attain curule office was so designated.

persons and in conformity with the provisions of the Licinian Law[1] of 367. The senate made common cause with the wealthy occupiers in defence of their prescriptive rights; Tiberius set in motion against them the legislative supremacy of the popular assembly and the powers of veto[2] vested in the tribunate, both of which had long been practically in abeyance, and a deadlock resulted. His agrarian law was passed, and a commission of three elected to put it in force, but Tiberius lost his life shortly after in an attempt to secure his re-election to the tribunate.[3]

The struggle, which had now become clearly defined as one between senate and people, was renewed on a larger scale by Tiberius' brother, *Gaius Gracchus*, in his first tribunate (123). Besides attempting to solve the economic problem by a system of colonization overseas, Gaius carried several important measures directly aimed at weakening the power of the senate —notably a *lex de provinciis* designed to prevent favouritism by the senate in allocating provinces, and a *lex iūdiciaria* which transferred the control of the court[4] which tried cases of extortion in the provinces (*quaestio de repetundis*) from the senate to the *equites*.[5] In order to enlist the support of every available ally, Gracchus further came forward with proposals for the enfranchisement of the Italian allies, which was destined to become more and more an acute question in Roman politics. The senate endeavoured to outbid him by the counter-proposals of *M. Livius Drusus*: Gaius, who had managed to secure his election to the tribunate for a second time (where his brother had failed), was unsuccessful at a third attempt, and, like Tiberius, fell in a riot (121).

§ 23.　[1] See § 9 (c).　　　　　　　　　　　　　　　[2] *Intercessio.*

[3] This was a vital necessity for Tiberius, as he was bound to be attacked when he had ceased to be protected by the 'sacrosanctity' of his office, § 9. He had acted unconstitutionally in deposing a colleague who attempted to veto his agrarian law.

[4] This was a very important measure and a great bone of contention afterwards.

[5] The *equites* of the Gracchan period were the rich merchants and financiers: their organization as the *equester ordo* may be said to date from C. Gracchus.

§ 24. Marius and Jugurtha

The agrarian reforms introduced by the Gracchi did not long survive them, but the struggle between the senate and the popular party, to which they had given rise, was continued along other lines. A notable success was scored by the *populares* in securing for *Gaius Marius*, a true son of the people, in preference to *Q. Metellus*, the aristocratic nominee of the senate, the command in the war against *Jugurtha*—a miserable quarrel into which Rome had been drawn in connexion with the division of the realm of the Numidian king Masinissa.[1] After a campaign of varying fortune, owing to the incompetence or corruption of the representatives of the senate, Jugurtha was subdued, largely through the instrumentality of *L. Cornelius Sulla*, who served as quaestor with Marius, and brought prisoner to Rome (106).

Marius, who had been elected consul a second time in his absence, covered himself with still greater glory by his victories over the barbarian hordes of the *Teutŏnes* and *Cimbri*, the former of whom were annihilated at *Aquae Sextiae*[2] (Aix) (102) and the latter at *Vercellae*[3] (101). Marius, who was now consul for the fifth time, celebrated a brilliant triumph, and the popular party had now not merely a determined tribune but a successful general, backed with all the power of the *imperium*, to champion their cause.

§ 25. Marius and Saturninus

The five consulships of Marius, though no doubt a triumph for the popular party, foreshadowed the menace which a general at the head of a victorious army might offer to the constitution. Marius, who was a better soldier than statesman, secured his election to the consulship for the sixth time (100), but he fell into discredit by his alliance with the demagogue *Saturnĭnus*, who as tribune introduced a series of popular measures on the

---

§ 24.   [1] § 14 (Third Period).
[2] In Gallia Narbonensis, north of Massilia.
[3] In the *Campi Raudii*, west of Milan.

lines of the Gracchan programme, and, like the Gracchi, met a violent death from which Marius was helpless to protect him (100).

§ 26. Livius Drusus the Younger

The death of Saturninus was followed by a temporary lull, and the next storm was to be provoked by proposals emanating from a party within the senate itself. The *equites* had abused the judicial powers conferred upon them by C. Gracchus; and *M. Livius Drusus*, son of the opponent of C. Gracchus, now (91) came forward with a proposal that the *iudices* should be chosen from the senate, which was to be increased from 300 to 600 by the addition of an equal number of *equites*. Coupled with his judicial reforms was apparently a scheme for the enfranchisement of the Italians. Neither of these measures found favour in the quarters which they affected, and in the violence of party feeling which they created Drusus was assassinated, and the senate pronounced his laws null and void.

§ 27. The Social War

For the moment the *status quo* was preserved: the *equites* retained control of the courts: but the Italians were determined to press for the enfranchisement which had so often seemed to be within their grasp and had as often been withdrawn. The death of Drusus brought matters to a head: the bulk of the Italian peoples, notably the Marsi, Samnites, Apulians, and Lucanians flew to arms, and the *Social War* began (91). The first year of the campaign was on the whole favourable to the allies, the next to the Romans, who were served by some distinguished generals; but Rome saw fit to introduce timely legislative concessions. By the *Lex Iulia* (90), the franchise was granted to those communities which had not joined in the revolt; this measure was supplemented the following year by the *Lex Plautia Papīria* which secured for the allies practically all they had demanded.

The enfranchisement of Italy from the Po[1] to the Straits of Messina was now complete; but the allies were to be enrolled in only eight out of the thirty-five tribes to prevent their swamping the old citizens. This arrangement was to become a burning question of Roman politics in the immediate future.

§ 28. Contest between Marius and Sulla: First Civil War

Both Marius and Sulla had served their country with distinction in the Social War: they were now to be sharply divided over the question of the command against *Mithridātes*,[1] king of Pontus, with whom Rome had come into conflict. The command was conferred on Sulla; but Marius coveted it and leagued himself with the tribune *P. Sulpicius Rufus*, who introduced measures for giving the charge of the war to Marius, and also for the distribution of the new citizens over the thirty-five tribes. As a result of these measures, which were carried with violence, Sulla led his army which was still besieging Nola[2] to Rome. Marius and Sulpicius fled:[3] the Sulpician laws were repealed, and Sulla sailed to take up his command, leaving as consuls for 87 *Cn. Octavius*, a representative of the senatorial party, and *L. Cinna*, a professed *popularis*.

§ 29. Marius and Cinna

No sooner was Sulla gone than Cinna revived the Sulpician programme respecting the distribution of the new citizens. An armed conflict between the consuls followed, in which Cinna was worsted and driven out of the city. Marius hastened from Africa to his support, and the two occupied Rome, where they proceeded to glut their revenge on their personal enemies, and

§ 27. [1] The *Lex Pompeia* (89) bestowed the 'Latin' franchise upon the Transpadanes: see also § 15 (v) (a).

§ 28. [1] This, the usual spelling, is probably less correct than *Mithradates*, which appears on coins.

[2] In Campania.

[3] The former made his escape to Africa, the latter was taken and put to death.

many distinguished men perished. Marius and Cinna then named themselves consuls for the following year (86—Marius' seventh consulship), but the former died not many days after.

§ 30. Sulla's Return: Second Civil War

For the next three years (86–84) Cinna was master of Rome, but the day of reckoning was approaching. Early in 83 Sulla, after arranging affairs in Asia, landed in Italy: Cinna, who had been preparing to oppose him in Greece, was murdered by his own troops, and Sulla met with but slight resistance. After wintering in Campania, Sulla defeated the younger Marius and shut him up in Praeneste: he then marched on Rome with his main force. The Samnites, who had joined the Marian party, were defeated in a bloody battle at the *Colline Gate*, and Sulla was master of Rome (82). The last efforts of the Marian party at resistance were stamped out by *Cn. Pompeius* in Sicily and Africa the following year; but *Sertorius* maintained himself in Spain for ten years (82–72).

§ 31. The Sullan Reforms

Almost immediately after his victory, Sulla had himself appointed dictator, and one of his first acts was the issuing of a *proscriptio* or list of personal enemies who might be put to death with impunity—a terrible precedent which was ever afterwards feared as a possible accompaniment of any political revolution.[1] The rebel communities in Italy were punished, and lands allotted to his veterans. By the beginning of 79 he had completed his constitutional reforms, whereupon he resigned his dictatorship. He died early next year (78).

The reforms of Sulla were embodied in the *Leges Corneliae*, which were far from being merely partisan in aim and were directed towards rehabilitating on a constitutional basis the rights which the senate had long exercised. With this object he had already, as consul in 88, made the *senatus auctoritas* necessary for proposals submitted to the assembly. He now:

§ 31.   [1] e.g. after Caesar's victory over Pompey.

(*a*) Restricted the wide powers of interference (*intercessio*) of the tribunate, and made the tenure of it a bar to the holding of any subsequent office.

(*b*) Re-enacted the *Leges Annāles*, requiring that the offices of state should be held in a fixed sequence—quaestorship, praetorship, consulship; and forbade tenure of the same office within a period of ten years. A senator could not begin his career in the senate before he was thirty.

(*c*) Encouraged the development of the promagistracy as the normal method of governing the provinces; by increasing the number of praetors he ensured a steady supply of ex-magistrates for the regular provinces.[2]

(*d*) Increased the number of quaestors to twenty, and made the quaestorship the qualification for entrance to the senate: the effect of this was practically to abolish the freedom of the censors in filling up vacancies, and to double the number of senators.[3]

(*e*) Extended the system of standing courts[4] (*quaestiones perpetuae*) for the trial of specific crimes, and to provide presidents for the new courts raised the number of praetors from six to eight. Further, the jurors (*iudices*) were to be chosen exclusively from the *senators* and not from the *equites*—a direct reversal of the law of C. Gracchus.[5]

The organization of the criminal courts was the most lasting part of his work; in politics the example of Sulla, revolutionary and autocratic as he was, proved to be more potent than the constitutional safeguards he enacted.

§ 32. Overthrow of the Sullan Constitution

The reformed constitution did not long survive its author. In 77, *Cn. Pompeius*, who had distinguished himself in the Sullan wars, was sent out to Spain with proconsular power, though he

---

[2] Sulla's eight praetors with the two consuls made up a total exceeding the maximum number of provinces requiring governors in any one year (§§ 21, 58).

[3] From this time the senate numbered about 600 members.

[4] Standing courts for extortion (*res repetundae*) and treason (*maiestas*) and perhaps others were already in existence.   [5] § 23.

had not even held the quaestorship, to conduct the war against *Sertōrius*, the Marian general,[1] who had organized a formidable resistance to Roman authority. Sertorius was treacherously murdered by a brother officer in 72, and Pompey returned in time to help *M. Licinius Crassus* to crush the slave rebellion headed by *Spartăcus* (71). Pompey and Crassus were elected consuls for 70, and a law introduced by Pompey restored in full the former powers of the tribunate, which had already ceased to disqualify for the higher magistracies by a *Lex Aurēlia* of 75. Another law of the same name proposed by the praetor *L. Aurelius Cotta* enacted that the juries for the criminal courts should be taken equally from among the senators, *equites*, and *tribuni aerarii*.[2]

§ 33. The Gabinian and Manilian Laws

The downfall of the Sullan constitution was complete, and Pompey stood forth as the great popular hero. But he was anxious for an important foreign command as the price of his

A COIN-PORTRAIT OF POMPEY
Photograph Ashmolean Museum

support, and he was soon rewarded by having the command against the pirates conferred on him by the *Lex Găbīnia* (67). The campaign against the pirates, who had terrorized the coasts of Italy and of the Mediterranean generally, was brilliantly conducted by Pompey, and he received in the following year the command against Mithridātes by the *Lex Mānīlia* (66), which Cicero supported in an extant speech. The exceptional powers conferred upon an individual by these two laws raised misgivings in the minds of more moderate

§ 32.   [1] § 30, end.
[2] Perhaps the order that came next to the *equites* in the *census*.

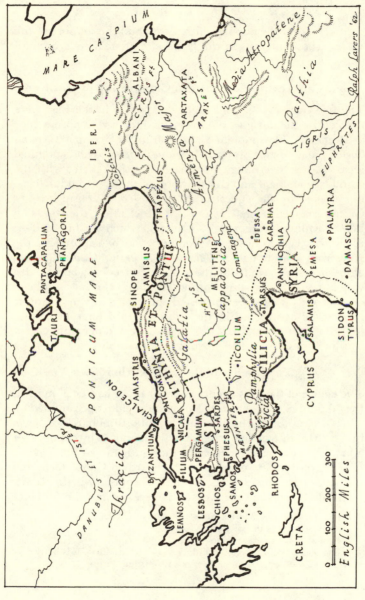

THE EAST IN THE TIME OF POMPEY

Ralph Lavers '62

politicians, but the popular enthusiasm and the support of the *equites*, whose interests in the East were at stake, overbore all opposition.

§ 34. Caesar and Cicero: the Conspiracy of Catiline

The five years (67–62) of Pompey's absence in the East were marked by the intrigues of Crassus and the rise to prominence at Rome of a new popular champion in the person of *C. Iulius Caesar*,[1] and of the orator *M. Tullius Cicero*, whose political ideal[2] was a government dominated by the senate, with the cordial attachment and co-operation of the great middle class represented by the equestrian order. Elected consul for 63,[3] Cicero satisfied vested interests by defeating the agrarian bill of Rullus (promoted by Caesar), which he branded as revolutionary and hostile to Pompey, and by suppressing the dangerous conspiracy of *Catiline* (*L. Sergius Catilīna*), who, after successive rebuffs at the consular elections, launched a violent revolutionary programme. Catiline's chief accomplices, *Lentulus* and *Cěthēgus*, were arrested and executed,[4] and Catiline himself fell fighting at the head of an armed force in Etruria (62). Both Caesar and Crassus were suspected of complicity in Catiline's designs, but their guilt is not established.

§ 35. The Struggle with Mithridates

The course of the past twenty years or more had been marked by a desultory war, which has been more than once alluded to, with *Mithridātes VI*, the able and ambitious monarch of *Pontus* in Asia Minor, who had extended his dominion by conquest or alliance over a wide territory to the south-east of the Euxine. A series of dynastic disputes with regard to Cappadocia and Bithynia precipitated the inevitable collision with Rome: Mithridates defeated the Roman forces, overran the province

§ 34.　[1] Nephew of Marius and son-in-law of Cinna.

[2] Expressed in the phrase *concordia ordinum*.

[3] Though a *novus homo*: the first since 94. § 22 A (ii).

[4] The question of the legality of the execution was afterwards hotly canvassed, and was destined to have serious results for Cicero.

of Asia, and ordered a great massacre of Romans and Italians throughout the cities (88). Mithridates, whose cause the Athenians had espoused, was encouraged to send his general

A CONTEMPORARY BUST OF CICERO. Vatican Museum

Archelāus with a large force into Greece, where Sulla landed in 87 and laid siege to Athens, which fell the following year. Sulla followed up his success by victories over Archelaus at *Chaeronēa* (86) and *Orchŏmĕnus*, and shortly after concluded a peace with Mithridates, whereby the latter was required to abandon his conquests in Asia and restrict himself to his own dominions (84). Sulla then returned to Greece, leaving his legate *L. Licinius Mūrēna* in charge of Asia. So ended the *First Mithridatic War*.

Murena, who presently found a pretext for invading

Mithridates' territory, was defeated by the king (82), but peace was renewed by the interposition of Sulla. This is sometimes known as the *Second Mithridatic War*.

Matters were brought to a head by the death of *Nǐcŏmēdes IV*, king of Bithynia, who bequeathed his dominions to Rome, whereupon they were declared a Roman province. Mithridates supported a claimant to the vacant throne and the struggle was renewed (74). (*Third Mithridatic War*.)

The operations on the Roman side were entrusted to the consuls *L. Licinius Lucullus* and *M. Aurelius Cotta*. Cotta was defeated by Mithridates, who laid siege to Cyzicus: here, however, he himself was besieged by Lucullus, who compelled him to retreat with heavy loss and carried the war into Pontus (73–72). Lucullus followed up his success by defeating *Tigrānes*, king of Armenia, Mithridates' son-in-law, with whom the latter had taken refuge, at *Tigranocerta* (69), and in the following year he pushed on towards *Artaxăta*. Lucullus' operations, however, were stopped by the mutinous attitude of his troops, and the two kings recovered their lost ground, till Lucullus was superseded by Pompey in 66 (*Lex Manilia*) as commander with extraordinary powers. Mithridates, after a defeat, made his way to the Cimmerian Bosphorus (Crimea), whither Pompey did not follow him, but addressed himself instead to the pacification of Armenia, which he successfully accomplished. *Pontus* (65) and *Syria* (64) were made Roman provinces, and next year (63) Pompey advanced still farther south and established Roman supremacy in Phoenicia, Coele-Syria, and Palestine. Here he heard of the death of Mithridates, who had been making extensive preparations for the renewal of the struggle (63). By the acquisition of Pontus, Bithynia, and Syria, Rome had enormously increased her territory and extended her rule to the Euphrates.

§ 36. The 'First Triumvirate'

Pompey landed in Italy in 62, and celebrated a splendid triumph the following year. Like Marius before, he was now called upon to exchange war for politics, and the former was more to his taste. For the moment the question of which political party he should join was dependent on two immediate objects—the ratification of his acts in Asia and a grant of land for his troops. Both were refused by the senate, and Pompey by force of circumstances was driven to make common cause with Caesar who had just returned from his pro-praetorship in Spain. The two, along with *Crassus*, whose immense wealth made him a useful ally, now entered into the compact known as the *First Triumvirate*[1] for the partition among them of the government of the Roman world (60). As soon as Caesar entered on his consulship[2] (59), he procured the ratification of Pompey's *acta*, and secured for the *publicani* the relief they had sought in vain from the senate in connexion with the taxes of Asia.[3] By a dexterous stroke Caesar had thus detached from the senatorial party both Pompey and the *equites*, but he still wanted an important military command to complete the strengthening of his position. This was soon forthcoming: a bill of the tribune *Vatinius* conferred upon him the command for five years (58–54) of Cisalpine Gaul and Illyricum, to which Narbonese Gaul was afterwards added. Here he would be able to keep in touch with events in the capital.

§ 37. Cicero and Clodius

Cicero's hopes of his ideal constitution were rudely shattered by the 'First Triumvirate', but more personal and immediate dangers were looming ahead. Cicero had made a bitter enemy of *P. Clodius Pulcher*, a man of notorious character, who, as tribune in 58, brought in a bill of pains and penalties against anyone who should be found to have put to death a Roman citizen untried. Cicero, who was obviously the object of attack, left in the lurch by Pompey, retired into exile in Greece, and a second law of Clodius pronounced him outlawed. Clodius, however, overshot himself by next attacking the triumvirs

§ 36. [1] It had no official character.

[2] His colleague was M. Bibulus, an aristocrat.

[3] Caesar relieved them of one-third of the lump sum they had undertaken to pay for the privilege of collecting these.

themselves, as they had now served his purpose against Cicero, and in order to thwart him Pompey actively exerted himself on behalf of the orator, who was recalled and returned to Rome amid acclamations (57).

§ 38. Renewal of the Coalition of Caesar, Pompey, and Crassus

On his return to Rome Cicero entertained fresh hopes of forming a strong constitutional party, but he was baulked by the obstinate opposition to the triumvirate of a section of the senate headed by *Cato*[1] and others. The reply of the triumvirs to these attacks was the renewal of the coalition by a conference at *Lūca*[2] (56), where it was arranged that Pompey and Crassus should be consuls for 55, while Caesar was to have his command prolonged for another five years. On entering upon office, the consuls procured the passing of a measure[3] giving the province of the two Spains to Pompey, and that of Syria to Crassus, each for a five-year period: the prolongation of Caesar's command was confirmed. Pompey elected to govern Spain by means of lieutenants, and remained at Rome: Crassus set out for his province before the end of 54, and next year (53) was defeated and killed in battle with the Parthians at *Carrhae* in Mesopotamia.

§ 39. Estrangement of Pompey and Caesar

The death of Crassus left the two ablest members of the coalition at the head of the state, and the course of events gradually forced them into mutual hostility. The series of brilliant victories in which Caesar had overrun Gaul (58–50) well-nigh eclipsed the triumphs of Pompey in the East, and the death of Julia[1] (54) severed the natural tie between the two. In these circumstances the bestowal upon Pompey of an extraordinary command for the preservation of order in connexion with the

§ 38.   [1] Great-grandson of the famous Cato the Censor.
[2] In Cisalpine Gaul: the point of Caesar's *provincia* nearest to Rome.
[3] *Lex Trebonia.*   § 39.   [1] Daughter of Caesar and wife of Pompey.

armed encounters between *Clodius* and *Milo*, in which the former lost his life, must have been very agreeable to his wishes. He was elected sole consul in 52, and had besides his provincial command prolonged for five years more. But these fresh powers brought him into close alliance with the senate, in which a powerful party was determined to make him head the attack upon Caesar.

§ 40. The Civil War

Caesar's command in Gaul technically expired on 1 March 49, but in the ordinary course of things he would not have a successor appointed to him till 1 January 48, and in the interval he desired to be a candidate for the consulship in his absence. His opponents in the senate were determined to appoint his successor on the legal expiry of his command, and so compel him to seek election as a private individual; or, if he retained his command, to prevent him from standing for the consulship. This was the main question in the discussions and negotiations of the years 51 and 50, which were marked by disingenuous shifts on the part of Pompey and bitter personal feeling on the part of the senate. After the resources of compromise had been wellnigh exhausted, Caesar made a final offer on 1 January 49 to resign his command if Pompey would do the same. The senate replied by declaring Caesar a public enemy unless he disbanded his army by a certain day, and by investing the consuls with dictatorial power.[1] Caesar crossed the Rubicon[2] and invaded Italy.

§ 41. Dyrrachium and Pharsalus

Caesar marched rapidly southward, and Pompey and his followers, who had resolved to quit Italy, barely managed to escape from Brundisium in time. Caesar, who was unable to follow him for want of ships, decided to secure Rome and the West before carrying the war eastward. Sicily and Sardinia,

§ 40. [1] § 55, n. 2.
[2] This was tantamount to a declaration of war.

important for the corn-supply, were occupied by his lieutenants; he himself brilliantly defeated *Afrānius* and *Petreius*, who held Spain for Pompey, and *Massilia* (Marseilles) was reduced after a siege. Meanwhile Caesar had been created dictator, but after a few days' tenure of the office he sailed from Brundisium in pursuit of Pompey and landed in Epirus (January 48). Failing to cut off Pompey effectively from his base at Dyrrachium, he resolved to blockade him, but Pompey broke through his lines, inflicting at the same time considerable loss on his opponent. Caesar now conceived the idea of drawing his enemy from his base by threatening his reinforcements from the East, and with this object started to march into Thessaly, whither Pompey followed him to be decisively defeated at *Pharsālus* (August 48). Pompey fled and gradually made his way to the coast of Egypt, where he hoped to find refuge with the young king Ptolemy,[1] and there in the act of landing he was treacherously murdered.

§ 42. Alexandrine, African, and Spanish Wars

Caesar, who had followed in pursuit, was drawn into a war on the question of the succession to the Egyptian throne, which he settled by establishing *Cleopatra* as queen after the defeat and death of her younger brother, Ptolemy, at the hands of the Romans (*Alexandrine War*). Later in the same year he defeated *Pharnāces*, son of the celebrated Mithridates, at *Zēla* (47);[1] and in the following year completely defeated the Pompeians in Africa in the battle of *Thapsus*. The last effort of the Pompeian resistance was crushed in the hard-fought battle of *Munda* in Spain (45). Caesar, who had celebrated his victories by a splendid fourfold triumph the previous year (46), had been voted further extraordinary honours from time to time: a second dictatorship and consulship and certain prerogatives of the tribunes were conferred upon him in 48; he was made dictator for ten years in 46, perpetual dictator in 44.

§ 41.   [1] Pompey had been instrumental in restoring his father to the Egyptian throne.

§ 42.   [1] In Pontus. With this victory was connected Caesar's famous dispatch to the senate: *veni, vidi, vici.*

§ 43. Caesar's Rule and Death

Caesar used his victory with moderation and soon dispelled the fears of those who anticipated a return of the Sullan régime. His victories had made him the supreme military head of the state; but in the scanty leisure allowed him from campaigning he had found time to effect several important social and administrative reforms, which were embodied in a series of *Leges Iuliae*. In March 49, by a *Lex Roscia*, he had conferred the full citizenship on the Transpadani, thus making Italy Roman up to the Alps. He enacted or drafted important laws which promoted the development of a uniform municipal system for the towns of Italy.[1] He raised the number of the senate to 900 by the introduction of new men, including some Gauls and Spaniards, on many of whose compatriots he conferred the franchise. An important reform of the calendar was also carried out.[2] Allotments of land in Italy, overseas colonization, schemes for the improvement of agriculture and for the draining of the Pomptine marshes figured among Caesar's numerous activities when he was cut off by a conspiracy among his personal friends, headed by *M. Brutus* and *C. Cassius*, 15 March 44.

Exactly what form of government Caesar would have evolved for the Roman world, had not death overtaken him so soon, it is perhaps hardly possible to say: as it was, he gathered up in himself all the elements of imperial rule which were more precisely defined by his successor Augustus. The title of *Imperator* which he assumed, his perpetual dictatorship, and the tribunician prerogatives, which were assumed in a more comprehensive manner and given greater emphasis by his successors, clearly assigned him a place above and beyond the constitution. To Augustus remained the task of discarding the more repellent of these forms[3] while retaining their substance, and of reconciling absolute power with republican traditions.

---

§ 43.　[1] The municipal system spread gradually over the western provinces, especially in Southern Gaul and Spain, through the initiative of Caesar and the emperors from Augustus onwards.

[2] See § 93.　　　　　　　　　　[3] e.g. the dictatorship.

§ 44. The Second Triumvirate

On the death of the dictator, *Marcus Antonius*, who had been his colleague in his last consulship, carried things with a high hand at Rome, professing to find authority for his acts in the late dictator's papers; but he had presently to reckon with an obstacle to his aggrandizement in the person of *C. Octavius* (Octavian), Caesar's great-nephew and heir, who appeared at Rome and was recognized by the senate (44). After a success against Antony, he demanded recognition as consul (43). This was followed by a law declaring the murderers of Caesar to be outlaws, and an agreement between *Antony*, *Octavian*, and *Lepidus*[1] for the division among them of the government of the Roman world for a period of five years.[2] Cicero, who had bitterly attacked Antony in his *Philippic* speeches, perished in the proscriptions which followed (43).

§ 45. Defeat of the Republicans

The position of the self-constituted triumvirs was not, however, unchallenged: *Sextus Pompeius*, son of Caesar's opponent, commanded the western Mediterranean with his fleet, while Brutus and Cassius had established a strong position in the East. Leaving Sextus alone for the moment, Antony and Octavian turned their attention to Brutus and Cassius, the campaign ending with the defeat and death of the republican leaders at *Philippi*[1] (42).

§ 46. Fresh Triumviral Arrangements

After the victory of Philippi, Antony undertook the task of restoring order in the East; Octavian charged himself with the settling of Italy and the prosecution of the war with Sextus Pompeius. A threatened rupture between the two was averted

---

§ 44. [1] *Magister equitum* at the death of Caesar and his colleague in the consulship (46).

[2] The arrangement was formally legalized by a *plebiscitum*.

§ 45. [1] In Macedonia.

OBVERSE AND REVERSE OF A COIN struck to commemorate the
assassination of Julius Caesar. Cap of liberty, daggers, and the date
'the Ides of March'

REVERSE AND OBVERSE OF A COIN. Julius Caesar deified
(divos Julius). Young Augustus 'divi filius'

ANTONY AND LEPIDUS

by the *Treaty of Brundisium* (40), which re-affirmed the division of the Roman world, Antony taking the East, Octavian Italy and the western provinces, while Lepidus, who had ceased to count, was given the single province of Africa. To seal the reconciliation, Antony married his rival's sister Octavia. In the following year Sextus Pompeius, who had been cutting off Rome's corn supply, was pacified by an arrangement known as the *Treaty of Misēnum* (39).

§ 47. Elimination of Pompeius and Lepidus

The agreement with Sextus did not last long: hostilities were renewed and ended in Sextus being decisively defeated at *Naulŏchus*[1] by Octavian's general, *Agrippa* (36). Pompeius fled to Asia Minor and was hunted down and put to death the following year. About the same time Lepidus, who had made a bid for recognition as an equal member of the triumvirate, was deprived by Octavian of his army and province, though his life was spared. Antony and Octavian were thus left face to face.

§ 48. Antony and Cleopatra

The successful termination of the war with Sextus Pompeius had been facilitated by yet another meeting of Antony and Octavian at Tarentum (*Treaty of Tarentum*), whereby the triumviral arrangement was extended for another period of five years (37–33). Antony spent several years organizing the Eastern provinces and vassal kingdoms, but his campaign against the Parthians was a failure (36) and his liaison with *Cleopatra* provided a handle for calumny and misrepresentation. The rupture with Octavian began when the latter failed to honour pledges made at Tarentum and was completed by Antony's divorce of Octavia. Outmanœuvred on the constitutional issue and challenged in February 32 by Antony's consul, Sosius, who accused him of illegally retaining his triumviral powers, Octavian replied with a *coup d'état* and a declaration of war, nominally against Cleopatra.

§ 47.   [1] On the north coast of Sicily.

§ 49. The War of Actium

Octavian was invested with a special war commission for the impending struggle, in which, like his great-uncle before him, he had the inestimable advantage of posing as the defender of Italy and the West against the East. Antony, who was at the head of very considerable forces, might have put a different complexion on the situation by invading Italy in 32: as it was, he allowed his fleet to be blockaded by Octavian in the Ambraciot Gulf,[1] while his land forces were useless against those of the enemy opposed to them. In the naval battle which followed, Cleopatra's squadron deserted in the heat of the action, and Antony followed her, despairing of victory. The rest of the fleet was destroyed; the land force surrendered a few days after. So ended the *Battle of Actium* (2 September 31 B.C.).

§ 50. Death of Antony and Cleopatra

Octavian did not pursue the fugitives to Egypt immediately, and in the interval Antony and Cleopatra had been endeavouring to repair their shattered strength. In the spring of 30, however, Octavian seized Pelusium and advanced on Alexandria. Antony, in despair at the desertion of his troops, which was increased by a false report of the death of Cleopatra, took his own life, and Cleopatra escaped the ignominy of gracing a Roman triumph by following his example. Egypt was now formally annexed as a Roman province. Octavian returned to Rome the following year and celebrated a triple triumph for his victories in Dalmatia, at Actium, and in Egypt. The temple of Janus[1] was closed for the third time in Roman history (29).

§ 51. The Principate

The victory of Actium had made Octavian master of the Roman world: it remained for him to consolidate and define the position he had won, and he brought to the task singularly

§ 49.   [1] In Epirus.

§ 50.   [1] This, which was really an archway (§ 89), was open in time of war, closed in time of peace.

suitable qualities of character and temperament. In January 27 B.C. he formally resigned the unconstitutional powers he had held as triumvir, and 'transferred the commonwealth into the keeping of the senate and people'. But he received in return even more ample powers than he had laid down. Along with his consulship, which he did not lay down, he was assigned the government of the more important military provinces for ten years with the power to make war and peace, and was authorized by decree of the senate to assume the surname *Augustus*.[1] His powers were further defined when he gave up the consulship in 23. His *proconsulare imperium* was declared superior to the *imperium* of all officers, both abroad (23) and at home (19); and the *tribunicia potestas*, on which he henceforth laid special stress as the emblem of his civil authority, was conferred on him for life.[2] The imperial provinces, in which large standing armies were needed, were governed by Augustus through lieutenants appointed by him and designated simply *legati Augusti pro praetore*, whilst the peaceful provinces were administered by the senate by means of governors who enjoyed the designation *pro consule*. In 12 B.C. on the death of Lepidus, Augustus succeeded him as Pontifex Maximus, so that henceforth he was also the religious, as well as the civil and military, head of the state.

Meanwhile, the senate continued to meet and the magistrates to discharge their customary functions, and the republic was spoken of as having been 'restored'. This was of course a convenient fiction which deceived no one. Beside the man who gathered up in his own person all the executive authority of the state, any other authority was out of the question. Augustus, however, studiously contrived to veil his autocratic power in constitutional forms, and chose, to designate his high position, the title *Princeps* or 'First Citizen'[3] in preference to 'dictator',

§ 51. [1] 'The Venerable' is perhaps the nearest equivalent.

[2] He had held tribunician *sacrosanctitas* since 36, and was offered the *potestas* in 29, but it was only now that it was given special prominence by Augustus.

[3] i.e. *princeps civitatis*, a term which Cicero had applied to both Caesar and Pompey.

which office had as a matter of fact been abolished by Antony, and was not revived by Augustus.

The character impressed on the Principate by the settlement

THE YOUNG OCTAVIAN (AUGUSTUS)
as ruler of the world, bearing the aegis of Zeus. An ancient cameo

of 23 B.C. was that which, in substance, it continued to maintain, and any changes were in the direction of autocracy. In two main respects a semblance of republican tradition was kept up: the Principate was never in theory strictly hereditary, though in practice it came to be regarded as such, and the new emperor was nominally invested by the senate and people between them with the prerogatives of his office.[4]

§ 52. Roman Emperors from Augustus to Marcus Aurelius

Augustus	27 B.C.–A.D. 14
Tiberius	14–37
Gaius (Caligula)	37–41
Claudius	41–54
Nero	54–68
Galba ⎫	68–69 ('Year
Otho ⎬	of the Four
Vitellius ⎬	Emperors')
Vespasian ⎭	
Vespasian ⎫	69–79 ⎫
Titus ⎬ Flavian Dynasty	79–81 ⎬
Domitian ⎭	81–96 ⎭
Nerva	96–98
Trajan	98–117
Hadrian	117–138
Antoninus Pius	138–161
Marcus Aurelius	161–180

§ 53. THE ROMAN CONSTITUTION

The original constitution of Rome has already been described (§ 5), and it has been seen how the monarchy was replaced by a republican form of government towards the close of the sixth century B.C. The break between the old and the new order of things was, however, less violent than might at first sight appear, and this was due to the conservatism of the Roman spirit which is traceable throughout the Roman political evolution. The consuls, for example, who replaced the king, were conceived as exercising each in his own right the full *imperium* or supreme executive authority which had belonged to the king; but it was now qualified by two important principles which characterized

---

[4] The *proconsulare imperium* was conferred by the senate, the *tribunicia potestas* by the people meeting in comitia.

the Roman magisterial system generally, viz. (*a*) the dual or collegiate character of the new office, whereby one consul could be a check on the other, (*b*) the restriction of the tenure of the office to one year. The Roman love for retaining old forms, while parting with the substance, is seen in the preservation of the kingly title for the officer known as *rex sacrorum* or *rex sacrificulus*. It has also been seen how successive magistracies owed their origin to the breaking-up process adopted by the patricians in their long struggle with the plebeians; and here again Roman conservatism was responsible for maintaining the new creations after they had ceased to serve their original purpose of staving off the attack on patrician monopoly. With these general principles in mind, we may proceed to notice in more detail the main elements in the fully developed Roman republican system—magistrates, senate, and public assemblies.

§ 54. Classification of Magistrates

The principal Roman magistrates may be classified in various ways:

(*a*) those who had and those who had not *imperium*, a term which signified the supreme executive authority, military, civil, and judicial, which was originally vested in the king, and which, in the case of a magistrate, implied particularly *the power to command an army*. The magistrates *with imperium* were: consul, praetor, dictator, magister equitum. *Without imperium*: censor, tribune, aedile, quaestor.

N.B. All magistrates had *potestas* or power sufficient to enforce the authority of their office.

(*b*) *Curule* or *non-curule*: a distinction which depended on the right to sit on the *sella cŭrŭlis*, a special chair of office. The non-curule magistrates were: tribune, plebeian aedile, quaestor.

(*c*) *Ordinary* or *extraordinary*: the extraordinary magistrates being the *dictator* and his *magister equitum* or 'second in command'.

The consuls and praetors—the only ordinary magistrates

with *imperium*—were attended by *lictors*[1] bearing the *fasces* or bundles of rods, symbolical of the power to flog. Consuls, praetors, censors, and curule aediles were distinguished also by the *toga praetexta*, bordered with a purple band.

§ 55. The Individual Magistracies

Consul. The consuls,[1] who had originally exercised jointly the full *imperium* of the kings, had their sphere gradually limited by the transference of some of their functions to other magistrates—censors, praetors, and aediles. After the institution of these, the main duties of the consuls were: (*a*) leading the armies in the field, in virtue of the *imperium* conferred upon them by a special vote of the people; (*b*) conducting the chief elections; (*c*) presiding in, and transmitting the orders of, the senate. When the censors went out of office, the consuls might succeed to their duties. Further, after the dictatorship had fallen into desuetude, the consuls, in grave state crises, might be invested by the senate[2] with dictatorial powers.

Praetor. The first praetor was appointed in 366 B.C. to take over the judicial functions of the consul. About 242 B.C. another was appointed to superintend cases in which a foreigner was concerned (*praetor peregrīnus*): the earlier was then styled *praetor urbānus*. The latter, or chief praetor, was the supreme civil judge of Rome, and the *edict* (*album*) which he published, setting forth the legal principles on which he intended to act during his year of office, became an important source of Roman law.[3] Praetors and ex-praetors, like consuls and ex-consuls, were regularly charged with the government of provinces, and their number increased with the number of the latter: e.g. two new praetors were required for Sicily and Sardinia (with Corsica),[4] 227 B.C.; two more for the Spains,[4] 197; and Sulla

§ 54. [1] Twelve in the case of the consul; the praetor had two in Rome, and six outside the city.

§ 55. [1] Their original designation was *praetores*, § 3, n.

[2] This was the *senatus consultum ultimum* which ran: *Videant consules ne quid res publica detrimenti capiat.*

[3] Through being adopted in substance by successive praetors.

[4] § 15.

ROMAN MERCHANT SHIPS OF THIRD CENTURY A.D. IN THE HARBOUR AT OSTIA
The lighthouse flame can be seen in the background

raised their number to eight in connexion with his establishment of the *quaestiones perpetuae*.[5] Under Caesar their number rose to sixteen.

Censor. The censorship was instituted in 443 B.C. The censors were two in number, elected about every five years, but they held office only for eighteen months. The censorship was regarded as the crown of a public career, and was usually held by an ex-consul. The chief functions of the censor were:

(*a*) to take the *census*, i.e. prepare the citizen list, and assess the property of each citizen for determining his status;

(*b*) to prepare the list of the senate;

(*c*) to manage the state finances.

In connexion with the first and second of these duties, the censor exercised wide powers of scrutiny in regard to the morals of the citizens; by affixing the *nota censoria* or 'black mark' to a man's name, they could degrade him from his tribe or his class. In the sphere of finance, they entered into contracts for the farming of the taxes and the construction of public works. Finally, before abdicating office, they conducted the *lustrum* or solemn ceremony of purification, a term which came to be applied to the five years' interval between the election of two successive sets of censors. The wide powers of the office were considerably contracted by the military reforms of Marius and the legislation of Sulla, which provided for the automatic recruiting of the senate from ex-quaestors.[6] The right of 'censure' was abolished by a law of Clodius in 58, and the office was finally absorbed by the emperors.

Aediles. The aediles were of two kinds, *plebeian* and *curule*. The former were two annual officers created at the same time as the tribunes of the plebs, whom they were intended to assist; in 367 B.C. two curule aediles (patrician) were appointed, nominally to superintend the public games: when the plebeians were admitted to the latter office, the functions of the two sets of officers became largely identical. The aediles had charge of the public buildings, of the cleansing and policing of the city,

[5] § 31. The praetors who presided in these courts were styled *quaesitores*.
[6] § 31 (*d*).

and controlled the markets. The regulation of the public games also fell largely within their province, and gave scope for lavish display to those looking forward to higher offices.

Quaestors. The quaestors were originally assistants of the consuls, and their duties from the first appear to have been connected with the treasury (*aerārium*). From the year 447 they were elected as magistrates at the *comitia tributa*. Originally two in number, they were increased in 421 to four, in 267 (probably) to eight, and in Sulla's time to twenty. In addition to two quaestors (*quaestores urbani*) who remained in Rome, attached to the treasury, a consul in the field was attended by one of these officers, who managed all financial affairs connected with the army, especially the sale of booty. Provincial governors were also assisted by quaestors as their financial agents.[7] The functions of the four *quaestores classici*,[8] at first connected with the fleet, were soon transferred to other departments (*provinciae*) —the most important of these being the *provincia Ostiensis*,[9] which supervised, among other things, the importation of corn.

Tribunes. The officers known as *tribuni plebis* were hardly magistrates in the same sense as the others, though in effect they had become such, and were regularly elected at the *comitia tributa*. Plebeians, naturally, alone were eligible for the office. The tribunate dated from the 'First Secession' (494), when two (perhaps five) members of the plebeian order were specially appointed to protect their order against the consuls:[10] the number was afterwards raised to ten. Their persons were inviolate (*sacrosancti*), and their chief power, in the later republic, was that of *intercessio*,[11] or putting a veto on the intended acts of all other magistrates (excepting a dictator) and even of one another.[12] This formidable power of the tribunate became one of the great instruments of political obstruction in the last century of the republic in the conflict between senate and people; but usually

---

[7] Cf. § 21.   [8] Appointed 267 (?).
[9] 'Department of Ostia', the port of Rome.   [10] § 9 (a) (ii).
[11] This grew out of their original *ius auxilii* or power to protect individuals from magisterial oppression. § 9 (a) (ii).
[12] The operation of the *intercessio*, though extensive, was not universal.

one member of the ten could be induced to veto the acts of his colleagues and so redress the balance. The prerogatives of the office were largely curtailed by Sulla,[13] but restored by Pompey.[14] The importance attached to them was shown by the fact that the *tribunicia potestas* was laid stress upon as an element in the power of the emperors.[15]

Dictator. The dictator, who appears frequently in the history of the early republic, was an occasional magistrate who was not elected, but nominated usually by a consul, on the recommendation of the senate. The dictator in turn nominated as his subordinate officer the 'master of the horse' (*magister equitum*): both held office for six months. The dictator superseded all other authority for the time being, and originally there was no appeal from him to the people.[16] The occasion of the appointment of a dictator might be a civil commotion, a quarrel between the consuls, or the expediency of placing the command of the army in the hands of a single individual. From the end of the Second Punic War the dictatorship was in abeyance: it was revived by Sulla in 82, and again by Caesar with much increased powers, but was subsequently abolished by Antony (44).[17]

§ 56. Election of Magistrates

The elections to the various magistracies were usually held about six months before the magistracies became vacant, which was normally the 1st of January. Between the date of his election and the date of his entering on office, a magistrate, e.g. a consul, was *consul dēsignātus* (consul elect). The higher magistrates (consul, praetor, censor) were elected by the *comitia centuriata*, presided over (usually) by a consul; curule aediles, quaestors, and inferior magistrates by the *comitia tributa*, presided over by a consul or the *praetor urbanus*; tribunes and plebeian aediles by the *comitia tributa*, presided over by a tribune.

---

[13] § 31 (*a*).   [14] § 32.   [15] § 51.
[16] This was allowed by a *Lex Valeria* of 300 B.C.
[17] § 51.

A PROCESSION OF MAGISTRATES, from a fourth century relief at Aquileia
Photograph Gabinetto Fotografico Nazionale, Rome

§ 57. The Cursus Honorum

The order in which the various offices might be held, and the requisite age for holding them, were probably fixed by the *Lex Villia Annalis* of 180 B.C. The quaestorship, curule aedileship, praetorship, and consulship had to be taken in this order: the plebian offices do not seem to have counted. The earliest age for holding the quaestorship appears to have been 28,[1] and as a clear interval of two years was required to elapse between the tenure of successive offices, a man might be aedile, praetor, and consul at 31, 34, and 37 respectively. In practice, however, the age seems to have been higher than the figures given; and under Sulla, who raised the age for the quaestorship to 30, the earliest age for the consulship would be 43. The holding of two offices together, or the holding of the same office within a space of ten years, was forbidden by statute, but the second of these provisions was frequently disregarded in state emergencies.

§ 58. Pro-Magistrates

The practice of continuing a magistrate in office beyond his legal term was as old as 327 B.C., when *Q. Publilius Philo*, after serving his year as consul, was retained in command of the

§ 57. [1] Ten years' military service, from the age of 17, was normally required as a qualification for office.

army for another year as pro-consul, by an extension (*prorogatio*) of his *imperium*; and a 'pro-magistrate' in the proper acceptance of the term meant a magistrate whose term of office had been so extended.[1] With the increase in the number of the provinces, however, when the regular magistrates of the year were not available as provincial governors, it became customary to invest with the imperium *pro consule* or *pro praetore* persons who had not held any magistracy at all, being thus qualified to exercise all the powers belonging to the special office, *but only outside Rome*. But from the time of Sulla, when the praetors were increased to eight, it became the normal practice (to which exceptions were infrequent) to furnish the provincial governors from the consuls and praetors who had first served their year of office in Rome.[2] This arrangement, however, was upset by a law of Pompey in 52, which required five years to elapse between the holding of a home and a foreign command, and thereafter a makeshift policy was adopted till order was established under the empire.[3]

FASCES. The axes and rods of the lictors

§ 59. THE SENATE

The senate under the republic was in theory no more than the purely advisory body it had been under the kings; it has been seen how, in effect, it became the real governing body in the state, with the magistrates deferring to its authority.[1] And it

§ 58.   [1] This was done originally by a decree of the senate and a vote of the people, afterwards by a decree of the senate alone.

[2] § 31 (*c*).   [3] § 51.   § 59.   [1] § 22.

must be admitted that this usurpation of power was on the whole justified by the use the senate had made of it in the best period of the republic.

THE CENTRE OF A LARGE ROMAN DISH, found in Switzerland in 1962
Photograph Elisabeth Schulz, Basle

The number of the senate, originally 100 and afterwards 300 under the kings, remained at the latter figure until the time of Sulla, who raised it to 600:[2] Julius Caesar increased it to 900, but it was reduced again to 600 under the empire.

The nomination of senators, which was made first by the

[2] § 31 (d).

kings and then by the consuls, was transferred by the *Lex Ŏvīnia* (351) to the censors, who, though theoretically free in their choice, were expected to give a preference to ex-magistrates. The censors' freedom of action was practically abolished by the reforms of Sulla, whereby the senate was automatically recruited from ex-quaestors.[3]

The chief departments in which the senate's authority was exercised may be enumerated as those of (*a*) legislation, (*b*) finance, (*c*) provincial administration, (*d*) foreign affairs, and (*e*) religion.

(*a*) Up till 339 B.C. (*Lex Publilia Philonis*) measures passed by the *comitia centuriata* were subject to the *patrum auctoritas*,[4] and *plebiscita* were not finally emancipated from senatorial control till the *Lex Hortensia* (287). But even after these restrictions had been removed, it was the regular custom for a magistrate to obtain the approval of the senate for a measure he was to introduce in the assembly. Moreover, a *senatus consultum* or decree of the senate, if in proper order,[5] and accepted by the magistrate who asked for it, though it had no legislative force in Republican times, was binding *de facto*.

(*b*) The censors and quaestors, the chief financial officers, were really dependent on the controlling body of the senate in all administrative questions of revenue and expenditure.

(*c*) The status of a province was usually defined under the direction of the senate, whose authority was paramount in the matter of provincial administration generally.[6]

(*d*) All foreign embassies were sent, and appeals addressed, to the senate. Decisions on peace and war required the sanction of the *comitia centuriata*, but here too the attitude of the senate was practically never questioned.

(*e*) The priests, not being magistrates, acted under direction of the senate, which took cognizance of all matters connected with religion, especially the admission of new deities and foreign rites. Isolated prerogatives of the senate were the continuance

---

[3] § 31 (*d*).   [4] For this expression see § 8, n. 3.

[5] If it was vetoed by a superior magistrate or tribune, it was a *senatus auctoritas*.   [6] Cf. § 21.

of a magistrate in office (*prorogatio imperii*), the granting of relief to individuals from the operation of certain legal restrictions (*solūtio legibus*), and the power of investing the consuls with dictatorial authority.[7]

§ 60. Procedure in the Senate

The senate could not initiate business except on the invitation of the magistrate (any other than quaestor) who summoned it to meet, and who was said *referre rem ad senatum*—to define the business for discussion. The meeting-place was generally the *Curia Hostilia*, but any *templum*, i.e. a place sanctioned by auspices, might serve the purpose. There seems to have been no fixed quorum, and an attendance of 400 members was probably considered a full meeting (*frequens senatus*), though senators were expected to be regular in their attendance. If the matter was one for debate rather than for an immediate vote, the president (who was the convening magistrate) called upon individual members to speak, which they did in order of precedence (*sententiam rogare: sententiam dicere*). There was no limit to the length of speeches, and 'talking against time' (*eximere* or *consumere diem dicendo*) was a common practice. Moreover, there was no bar to the introduction of matter irrelevant to the strict subject of debate.[1] A vote was taken by division (*discessio*), and voters were said *pedibus in alicuius sententiam ire*.[2] A vote of the senate, if in proper order and accepted, was known as a *senatus consultum*; if vetoed by a magistrate having the necessary authority, it was only a *senatus auctoritas* or expression of opinion.

[7] By the *senatus consultum ultimum*, § 55 (consul). But the senate's authority in this matter was strongly combated by the *populares* of the republic.

§ 60.   [1] Cf. the well-known anecdote of Cato the Censor who wound up every speech with *ceterum censeo delendam esse Carthaginem*.

[2] The precise significance of the term *pedarii*, usually understood of members who had the right to *vote* (*pedibus . . . ire*) but not to *speak*, is disputed.

§ 61. THE COMITIA OR POPULAR ASSEMBLIES

Under the republic we have to take account of three main citizen assemblies—the *comitia curiata, comitia centuriata,* and *comitia tributa.*

Observe (*a*) that the term *comitia*[1] means properly a meeting of *the whole citizen body*—patrician and plebeian alike—for voting purposes: contrast *comitia tributa,* a meeting of the whole people voting by tribes, with *concilium plebis,* a meeting of plebeians only.

(*b*)That the terms *curiata, centuriata, tributa* denote the various ways in which the same body, practically, voted for particular purposes: in the first case the voting was 'by *curiae*', in the second 'by *centuries*', and in the third 'by *tribes*', i.e. the voting was by *groups,* not by *heads,* and the majority of individual votes within the voting-group determined the vote of the group.

(i) The *comitia curiata,* which had originally conferred the *imperium* on the king,[2] was in republican times but a shadow of its former self,[3] and continued to meet only for certain formal purposes, such as the conferring of the *imperium* on consuls and praetors.

(ii) The *comitia centuriata* as organized by Servius Tullius has already been described.[4] The centuries of the first class voted first, lots being cast to determine which of these should commence the voting (*centuria praerogātīva*). The centuries of the second class followed, and so on. The effect of the centurial arrangement in the original scheme had been to give the richest class an overwhelming advantage in voting; but a reform had been introduced somewhere about the middle of the third century B.C., the essence of which appears to have been the blending of the centurial system with the tribal. The details of the new scheme are uncertain. Possibly the co-ordination of centuries with tribes was not carried lower than the

---

§ 61.   [1] The singular *comitium* signifies the meeting-place of a *comitia,* and was used specially of a space adjoining, or sometimes reckoned part of, the Roman Forum.   [2] § 5.

[3] It was represented only by magistrates and lictors.   [4] § 7 and § 8 with n. 2.

second class, the first class being given 70 centuries, the second 35 out of the total of 193 retained from the Servian system. The result of the reform would be to allow the second class as well as the first an effective voice in determining the voting.

Functions. The *comitia centuriata* (*a*) elected the higher magistrates (consul, praetor, censor); (*b*) decided on peace and war, though in practice this power was often usurped by the senate;[5] (*c*) acted as a court of appeal from the sentence of a magistrate in criminal cases (*Lex Valeria de provocatione* (509),[6] re-enforced 449 and 300). Being theoretically an assembly of the army,[7] the *comitia centuriata* could be summoned only by a magistrate with *imperium* (dictator, consul, praetor), and could not meet inside the city.

(iii) The existence of a *comitia tributa*, i.e. an assembly of the whole people voting by tribes and summoned by consuls and praetors as well as by tribunes, is established from the middle of the fifth century B.C. The precise relation of this assembly to the *concilium plebis*, a meeting of the plebeian body presided over by a plebeian magistrate, is difficult to determine, and cannot be discussed here.

Functions. The *comitia tributa* (*a*) elected the inferior magistrates (tribunes, quaestors, aediles); (*b*) judicially, it took cognizance of appeals in certain cases where capital punishment was not involved; (*c*) steadily increased in importance as a source of Roman *legislation*.

N.B.—The *comitia centuriata*, *comitia tributa*, and *concilium plebis* all had *legislative* powers, and the enactments of all three bodies were on the same footing in respect of validity after the *Lex Hortensia* of 287.[8] The term *lex* was strictly applicable only to resolutions of the first and second; those of the third were properly known as *plebiscita*. In practice, however, the name had become a matter of indifference, and many important 'laws' were *plebiscita* proposed by tribunes. Under the empire, the functions of the *comitia* were much restricted: Tiberius transferred the election of magistrates to the senate. The *comitia*

---

[5] § 59 (*d*).
[7] Cf. § 7, n. 5.

[6] § 9 (*a*) (i).
[8] See § 9 (*b*) (iv).

tributa occasionally passed laws and conferred the *tribunicia potestas* and other prerogatives on the new emperor.[9]

§ 62. ROMAN LAW AND LAW COURTS

In early times, when law was mainly what was sanctioned by use and wont, the king was the sole judge of the community. His judicial powers passed to the consuls who exercised them with the same wide discretion; but an important advance was made with the publication in the middle of the fifth century B.C. of the famous *Twelve Tables*, which were regarded ever after as a great legal charter. Other sources of law under the republic were: (*a*) *senatus consulta*, if passed in proper form;[1] (*b*) enactments of the various legislative assemblies, which all had the force of *leges* after 287 B.C.; (*c*) edicts of magistrates, especially of the praetors, concerning matters coming within the purview of their respective offices.

In the matter of *jurisdiction*, i.e. power to administer the law, this was possessed to a certain extent by every magistrate in cases appertaining to his office.[2] But the great bulk of civil cases came within the province of one or other of the praetors—the *praetor peregrīnus*, who had jurisdiction in all disputes between citizens and non-citizens (*peregrini*), and the *praetor urbānus*, who was the supreme civil judge of Rome, though he did not usually try the facts of a case himself.

A. *Procedure in Civil Cases*

The plaintiff in a civil case might proceed either (*a*) *per legis actionem*, or (*b*) *per formulam*, both under direction of the praetor. By the first, he had to raise his claim in one or other of several definitely prescribed legal forms in the exact words of the Twelve Tables: the praetor, after satisfying himself that all technicalities had been observed, usually sent the case to be tried by a *iūdex*. The rigidity of this system, which naturally did

---

[9] § 51, n. 4.   § 62. [1] 59 (*a*) and n. 5.
[2] e.g. the censors in matters of taxation, the quaestors in treasury cases, and so forth.

A ROMAN SENATOR; a marble statue in the Museo Capitolino, Rome

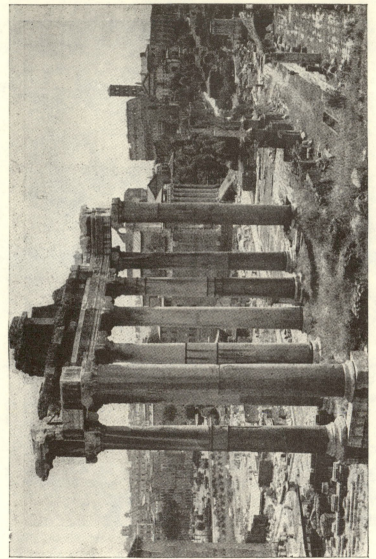

THE ROMAN FORUM
Photograph Bradford

not provide for many cases that might easily arise, led to its being superseded almost entirely by the procedure *per formulam*, the *formula* being a general instruction, adapted to the needs of the case, to the *iudex* or *arbiter* or *recuperātōres* to whom the praetor sent the case for trial. The 'formulary' system consisted of two parts: (*a*) *in iure*; (*b*) *in iudicio*.

(*a*) *in iure*. The plaintiff summoned the defendant (*vocavit in ius*), and the two parties made an appointment (*vadimōnium*), under guarantees, to appear before the praetor on a proper day (*dies fastus*). The praetor, after hearing both sides, granted a *formula* (i) appointing a judge, (ii) stating the case to be argued, (iii) directing the judge as to damages. The formal words with which the praetor granted the *formula*, viz. *do, dīco, addīco*,[3] were known as the *tria verba*.

(*b*) *in iudicio*. The actual trial was conducted before the *iudex* or *recuperatores* by sworn evidence. The defendant might, of course, throw up his case at any stage of the proceedings; if he lost, he was allowed thirty days in which to pay the damages, the execution of the judgement being left, in the first instance, to the parties themselves. In the system of *legis actiones* the plaintiff had to conduct his own case, but under the formulary system he might be represented by an agent (*prōcūrātor*), and might have professional lawyers or orators (*advocati, patrōni, causidici*) to plead for him at the trial.

B. *Procedure in Criminal Trials*

By the *Lex Valeria de provocatione* (509) a prisoner condemned on a capital charge was allowed to appeal from the consul to the *comitia centuriata*; and by the *Lex Aternia Tarpeia* (454) a prisoner condemned by any magistrate to a fine exceeding a certain amount was allowed an appeal to the *comitia tributa*. As such appeals were made as a matter of course, the comitia became the great criminal tribunals, the *comitia centuriata*

---

[3] i.e. *do iudicium* ('I grant a trial'); *dico ius* ('I declare the law'); *addico litem* ('I assign the matter in dispute'). The last was really applicable only to the time when the praetor decided a case himself.

dealing especially with cases of murder (*parricīdium*) and treason (*perduellio*). The accusing magistrates were, in the case of the *comitia centuriata*, the consul or his delegates,[4] in the case of the *comitia tributa*, the tribunes or aediles.

The *Quaestiones Perpetuae*

The inconvenience of such a large body as the *comitia* inquiring into a complicated case gradually led to its delegating its jurisdiction to a special commission (*quaestio*), presided over by some magistrate with *imperium*. A permanent court of this nature for the trial of extortion cases (*de repetundis*) was first instituted in 149 B.C., and Sulla increased the number to at least seven,[5] each dealing with a special offence, e.g. *de ambitu* ('bribery'), *de falso* ('fraud'), &c. These new standing courts (*quaestiones perpetuae*) were presided over by a praetor,[6] who in this capacity was a *quaesītor*, failing whom by a specially appointed *iudex quaestionis*, who was often an ex-aedile. The jurors (*iudices*) in courts of this kind were, under C. Gracchus, *equites*;[7] Sulla reinstated senators;[8] by the *Lex Aurelia* of 70 they were drawn equally from senators, *equites*, and *tribuni aerarii*.[9]

Procedure before a quaestio. The usual procedure before a *quaestio* was as follows: The accuser denounced the accused before the president of the proper *quaestio* (*nomen detulit*): if several accusers came forward, one was selected by a preliminary examination (*dīvinatio*) to act as chief accuser,[10] and was required to conduct the case in a straightforward manner. A day was then fixed for the trial, which, if not finished on the first day, was adjourned to the next but one (*compĕrendīnatio*). When evidence and arguments were over, the jury were called upon to vote, which they might do either orally or by ballot, the votes, in the former case, being *absolvo* ('I acquit'), *condemno* ('I convict'), or *non liquet* ('not proven'). For voting by ballot

---

[4] The *quaestores parricidii* or *duoviri perduellionis*.   [5] § 31 (*e*).

[6] Other than the *p. peregrinus* or *urbanus* who were of course occupied with *civil* cases.

[7] § 23.   [8] § 31 (*e*).   [9] § 32 (end).

[10] The rest became his *subscriptores* or 'backers'.

each juryman had a ticket, marked on one side with A (*absolvo*), on the other with C (*condemno*), one or both of which letters he erased before dropping the ticket in the urn (*sitella*). The ordinary penalties were either a fine (*multa*), loss of citizenship, or exile. There was no appeal from the verdict of a *quaestio*.

§ 63. THE ROMAN ARMY

A. EARLIEST PERIOD. The original army of Rome was the *lĕgio* or 'muster' of 3,000 citizens, arranged in three regiments of 1,000 each, each under the command of a special officer (*tribunus militum*): the whole army was commanded by the king. In addition to the infantry, there was a body of 300 cavalry, divided into ten squadrons (*turmae*) of thirty men each, and each squadron containing three bodies of ten each (*decuriae*). This early force appears to have been exclusively patrician. The term *legio* continued throughout history to denote the largest Roman military unit, which varied in number from time to time within moderate limits, seldom falling below 3,000, and rising, from the time of Marius, to 6,000 or 6,200. The 300 cavalry, however, continued to be the normal complement of the legion.

B. THE REFORMS OF SERVIUS TULLIUS. The *comitia centuriata* as instituted by Servius Tullius was, as has been seen,[1] really a reorganization of the army, every citizen being required to serve in a rank proportionate to his property. The richest served as cavalry with horses furnished by the state (*equites equo publico*); those of the first class who were not rich enough to serve as cavalry, formed the heavy infantry, with a full suit of armour;[2] the equipment of the remaining classes being less and less in proportion to their rating. The footsoldiers formed four legions, two of *iuniores* (17–45) and two of *seniores* (46–60). The first three classes fought in phalanx formation, with a frontage

§ 63.   [1] § 7.
[2] Helmet (*galea*), cuirass (*lōrīca*), greaves (*ocreae*), round shield (*clipeus*), and lance (*hasta*).

of 500 men and a depth of six ranks, the two lowest classes fighting alongside as light-armed troops (*rōrarii, ferentarii*).[3]

C. The Manipular System: Fourth–Second cents. b.c.

The Servian phalanx must have been somewhat unwieldy and ill-adapted to anything but a frontal attack. At any rate, by the time of the Latin War[4] (340 B.C.) the phalanx had been replaced by a new formation, in which the tactical unit was the 'maniple' (*manipulus*). Under the fully-developed manipular system, the legion was drawn up in three lines as follows:

$$\left\{ \begin{array}{l} \text{1,200 } hast\bar{a}ti \text{ (young men)} \\ \text{1,200 } principes \text{ (men in their prime)} \\ \text{600 } tri\bar{a}rii \text{ (older and more experienced)} \end{array} \right.$$
formed the 1st line;
,,   ,, 2nd ,, ;
,,   ,, 3rd ,, .

1,200 *vēlĭtes* (youngest and poorest citizens), who acted as skirmishers, made up the normal legion of 4,200. When the legion numbered more than 4,200, the additional troops were distributed among the *hastati*, *principes*, and *velites*: the *triarii* remained constant.

Each of the three lines was divided into ten *maniples* of two *centuries* each, so that the normal century of the *hastati* and *principes* was sixty men, that of the *triarii*, thirty. The complement of 300 cavalry was drawn up in ten *turmae* of thirty men each.

N.B.—The above arrangement must have been the outcome of a gradual series of changes, as is shown by the phraseology: the *triarii*, who were also styled *pīlani*, were armed not with the *pīlum* but with the *hasta*, while the *hastati* and *principes* carried *pila*. Also the *principes*, in spite of their name, formed not the *first* but the *second* line.

Method of fighting. The attack was begun by the *velites*, who ran forward and threw their missiles, and then retired through openings left between the maniples, which, during the skirmishing, were usually arranged in *quincunx* form ($:\cdot:$): when the action developed, these openings were probably filled up and

---

[3] The poorest citizens (*capite censi*) were usually exempted from service.
[4] § 10 (Fourth Period).

the lines made continuous. On approaching to close quarters, the *hastati* hurled their *pila* and then engaged with the sword: if the *hastati* were defeated, the *principes* advanced. The *triarii* were a last reserve and were not normally called upon.[6]

D. The Cohortal System: from Marius till the end of the Republic. The military reforms of Marius[7] may be said to have impressed upon the Roman army the character which it continued to bear, substantially, throughout subsequent history, both as regards conditions of service and disposition in the field. Under Marius, free birth, irrespective of age or wealth, was made the sole qualification for service in the legion and the older method of citizen levies for a single campaign was largely replaced by voluntary enlistment for the term of command of an individual commander. With regard to the legion, the old classes of *hastati, principes*, and *triarii* disappeared, and all legionaries bore the same equipment, the *hasta* being discarded for the *pīlum*, which was carried by all. The tactical unit was now made the *cohort (cohors)*, which was a combination of three maniples,[8] and each maniple was in turn divided into two centuries, a *prior* and a *posterior*, each commanded by a centurion. The number of cohorts was always ten, their strength thus varying with the strength of the legion, which now averaged 6,000 men.[9] The legion now received a standard, a silver eagle (*aquila*), soon came to be distinguished by a permanent number, and began to have a corporate history.

§ 64. Recruiting

A levy (*dīlectus*) was held each year by the consuls for the purpose of enrolling the four legions which were normally raised. A tribe was chosen by lot, and from it four members, with

---

[6] Hence the proverbial expression, *res ad triarios rediit*, of a critical situation.

[7] §§ 24 ff.

[8] The old *names* were retained for these sub-divisions of the cohort, which were known as *pilani* (*triarii*), *principes*, and *hastati* respectively.

[9] In a battle the number probably did not exceed 4,000.

names of good omen, were called, and assigned one to each of the four legions. Other names were then called, four at a time, till the tribe was exhausted; and so with the other tribes till the legions were completed. After the levy the troops took the military oath (*sacrāmentum*), which was binding while the general to whom it was taken remained in command. From the time of Marius the oath was taken for the term of military service. Under the empire the oath became one of allegiance to the emperor, and was taken twice annually.[1]

§ 65. Socii and Auxilia

As the dominion of Rome was enlarged, the allied communities, as well as the full citizens, furnished material for the Roman army, the quota to be supplied by each being fixed by the consuls, while the communities themselves enrolled the troops, Rome finding their rations in the field. The contingents of the allies (*socii*) formed the wings (*ālae*) of the legions and consisted both of infantry and cavalry, in the proportion usually of 10,000 foot and 1,800 horse to a consular army of two legions. The command of these allies was vested in six Roman officers (*praefecti socium*) appointed by the consul. After the Social War (89 B.C.)[1] the *socii* naturally disappeared as a distinct force and were incorporated in the legions.

From the *socii* must be distinguished the *auxilia* or *auxiliāres*, who were foreign mercenaries, serving usually as cavalry or as light-armed troops (*levis armātūra*). Roman cavalry proper, which had never been a very effective force, had ceased to exist by the first century B.C., and Italian cavalry was not employed after the Social War. From this time forward this arm was represented by foreign nationalities, Gauls, Spaniards, and Africans. The light-armed troops were usually chosen for their skill in the use of some national weapon, e.g. the Balearic slingers, Moorish dartmen &c.

§ 64.   [1] On the 1st of January and on the anniversary of the emperor's accession.

§ 65.   [1] § 27.

§ 66. Officers

A Roman army, in republican times, was commanded by a general with *imperium*—usually a consul (or dictator) or praetor (or proconsul, propraetor). Under the empire the emperor was the supreme commander of all the forces, and all victories were his as being won under his *auspicia*.

The infantry of each legion was commanded by six tribunes: twenty-four of these were thus required for the four legions that were normally raised, and were all elected by the people (after 207 B.C.). Under Caesar a special officer of ripe experience, called *lēgātus legionis*, was appointed to each legion, a practice which was followed under the empire, and the office of the legionary tribune, though maintained, became less responsible.

Of the subordinate legionary officers by far the most important were the sixty *centurions*, at the head of whom stood the *prīmus pīlus* or *prīmipīlus*, i.e. the senior centurion of the first cohort in the legion. A strict order of seniority was observed among the *primi ordines*, the centurions of the first cohort, but below these there was no important difference in rank among the six centurions of each cohort. Hence, a centurion's promotion was usually from cohort to cohort, often with a change of legion, until he entered the *primi ordines*. These were, in ascending order of rank, *hastatus posterior, hastatus prior, princeps posterior, princeps prior, pilus posterior, pilus primus.*

The centurions were the chief professional officers of the legion and the backbone of the Roman army. The centurion carried a vine-staff (*vītis*), suggestive of the disciplinary duties of his office.

§ 67. Standards and Standard-Bearers

Among the minor legionary officers were the various classes of standard-bearers (*vexillarii, aquiliferi, signiferi*). The *vexillum* was a small red flag: displayed over the general's tent, it was the

A ROMAN INFANTRYMAN

signal for battle: it was also the ensign of the legionary horse and of special detachments.

The silver eagle (*aquila*) was the standard of the legion,

AQUILIFER

introduced in the time of Marius to replace previous emblems. The *signum*, a silver-plated pole, variously adorned, was the ensign of the legionary cohort. Besides the standard-bearers may be mentioned trumpeters (*tŭbĭcĭnes*) and horn-blowers (*cornĭcĭnes*),[1] corporals who passed the watchword (*tesserarii*), artisans (*fabri*), and orderlies (*optiones*) of various kinds.

§ 68. Dress, Weapons, Armour, &c.

(*a*) The body of the legionary soldier was protected by a leather doublet (*lōrīca*), some-times strengthened with plates of metal. Under this was worn a close-fitting woollen tunic, reaching nearly to the knees. His feet were shod with hob-nailed boots (*călĭgae*), fastened with thongs. His legs were usually bare, but in cold climates they might be protected by short breeches (*brācae*), such as were worn by the Gauls, or by leg-bandages (*fasciae*). He had also a cloak (*săgum*) of brownish stuff, reaching to the knees: the long cloak

§ 67.   [1] The *tuba* was the straight infantry trumpet; the *cornu*, as the name suggests, was curved.

(*pălūdāmentum*), usually of scarlet, was the distinguishing dress of the Roman general.

(*b*) The defensive armour consisted of a helmet, first of leather (*gălea*), and later of metal (*cassis*); a greave (*ocrea*), worn on the right leg; and a rectangular shield (*scūtum*), of leather, with iron rims at top and bottom, measuring about four feet by two and a half. The *scutum* was cylindrical in shape, so as to cover the body, and usually had a large boss (*umbo*) of bronze or iron in the centre.

(*c*) The offensive weapons were (i) the short Spanish sword (*glădius*), about two feet long, suited for stabbing rather than cutting. It was worn on the right side, either hung from a baldric (*balteus*) or more often fastened to a metal-plated waist-belt (*cingulum*); (ii) the javelin (*pīlum*), two of which were carried by each legionary. This could be used either for thrusting or throwing, and measured about seven feet over all. The head, which formed about one-third of the total length, consisted of a piece of soft iron, which bent on impact, and so was useless for throwing a second time.

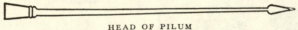

HEAD OF PILUM

The early legionary cavalry were equipped with a leather corslet, iron helmet, and light round shield (*parma*), and carried a lance (*hasta*), javelins (*vĕrūta*), and a sword.

(*d*) On the march, the legionary carried, in addition to his weapons and armour, a kit (*sarcĭnae*),[1] consisting of clothes, cooking vessels (*vāsa*), rations (*cĭbus, cĭbāria*) for so many days, as well as entrenching tools and two stakes (*sŭdes, valli*).

(*e*) The rations of the Roman soldier consisted chiefly of wheat (*trītĭcum*), which was served out unground, at the rate of one bushel per month. The soldiers ground it in hand-mills, and made either bread or porridge (*puls*). The chief drink was a sour wine (*posca*).

(*f*) Pay (*stīpendium*) was introduced in 406 B.C. In the second

§ 68.   [1] The plural is regular in this sense.

century B.C. this seems to have been on a scale of 120 *denarii* annually for the legionary, centurions receiving twice, and horsemen three times, as much. Under Caesar the scale was raised to 225 *denarii* paid in three instalments. Of the scale for higher grades, little is known; the legionary tribunes, at least in republican times, appear to have received nothing. Besides their ordinary pay, soldiers would occasionally receive a share of booty (*praeda*), while the emperors usually distributed large bounties (*dōnātīva*) at their accession or in their wills.

(*g*) Various distinctions were awarded for acts of bravery. The highest of these was the crown of oak leaves (*cŏrōna cīvĭca*), for saving the life of a fellow-soldier in the field. Crowns were also awarded to those who were the first to scale an enemy's walls or enter his camp (*coronae mūrāles, castrenses*). Other decorations for distinguished service were *phălĕrae* (round embossed plaques of metal), armlets (*armillae*), and necklets (*torques*). A soldier was also rewarded by exemption from certain duties, increase of pay, or promotion in the service.

§ 69. Order of March

The order of march naturally depended upon circumstances. As a rule, the legions marched in column (*agmen*), each legion with its baggage (*impĕdīmenta*)[1] following, the cavalry acting as a guard on flanks or rear. If the enemy were near, several legions might be sent on in advance ready for action (*legiones expedītae*[2]): behind these came the whole of the baggage: the rest of the troops closed the rear (*claudere agmen*). If this formation was strengthened by a covering column for the baggage on either flank, as was done in dangerous situations, the result was a hollow square (*agmen quadrātum*). The advance in order of battle would be adopted only for a short distance and when

---

§ 69. [1] This, the heavy baggage, tents, &c., carried in wagons or by beasts of burden, must be distinguished from the soldiers' packs (*sarcinae*).

[2] This term was used of men or units who had discarded the heavier part of their equipment for greater mobility: hence *expediti milites, expeditae cohortes*, &c.

an immediate attack was expected. An ordinary day's march (*iter*) would average from fifteen to twenty miles; forced marches (*longa* or *magna itinera*) might be much longer.

§ 70. Order of Battle

The tactics under the manipular system have been already described.[1] In the cohortal system, as developed by Caesar in his campaigns in Gaul, the legion was usually drawn up in three lines of cohorts, with an interval between each cohort, in such a way that, of the ten cohorts, four formed the first line, three the second, and three the third, the intervals in the first line being covered by the cohorts of the second line, thus:[2]

IV	III	II	I
VII	VI	V	
X	IX	VIII	

When, as was usually the case, several legions were engaged together, these would be arranged side by side so as to form a continuous front. The normal depth of each line was probably eight men.[3]

The attack was delivered, as a rule, only by the first line of cohorts, who, charging at a run, delivered their *pila* and then attacked with the sword; if this was not decisive, they were relieved by the second line, which advanced and took their places either by a flank movement or by passing through the intervals in the first line. The first line might in turn relieve the second: the third was held in reserve. The brunt of the attack was borne by the infantry, the cavalry being employed either to protect the flank of the former[4] or to check the enemy's

§ 70.   [1] § 63 C.

[2] This was the regular *triplex acies*: Caesar, however, sometimes employed a *duplex*, and once at least a *simplex, acies*.

[3] Pompey's arrangement of his cohorts *ten* deep at Pharsalus is mentioned as being exceptional.

[4] Especially the right, which was not protected by the shield (*latus apertum*).

horse or light-armed troops. If the enemy were victorious, the retreat was sounded (*receptui canere*), and the legions fell back (*pedem referre, se recipere*) on their fortified camp.

Besides the ordinary frontal attack, sometimes the right wing (*dextrum cornu*) might move forward first, sometimes the left (*sinistrum cornu*); sometimes both wings might advance together, the centre holding back (*sinuata acies*), or the centre (*media acies*) advanced in a crescent or wedge-formation (*cŭnĕus*), designed to pierce the enemy's line. Sometimes a formation presenting a front all round (*orbis*) was adopted to prevent being surrounded by superior numbers.

§ 71. Camp

A Roman army on halting for the night always proceeded to form a camp (*castra*), the site of which was carefully chosen and marked out by professional surveyors (*mensōres*), usually on the slope of a hill within reach of forage, wood, and water. A ditch (*fossa*) was first dug, enclosing a square;[1] inside the ditch a rampart (*agger*) was formed of the earth thrown up from the former, and strengthened by a palisade (*vallum*) of the stakes which the soldiers carried.[2] The camp had two main gates, the *porta praetōria* in the middle of the side facing the enemy, and the *porta dĕcŭmāna* on the side farthest away from them. There were also two side gates, the *porta principālis dextra* and the *porta principālis sinistra*, between which ran the *via principalis*, the main street of the camp, 100 feet wide, connected with the *porta praetoria* by the *via praetoria*, and dividing the square into two main portions. Of these the larger portion, between the *via principalis* and the *porta praetoria*, was further divided by a road called the *via quintāna*, running parallel to the *via principalis*, and here the main bulk of the legions and other troops was housed, ten men being allotted to a tent (*contŭbernāles*).

The hinder and smaller portion, between the *via principalis*

---

§ 71. [1] Under the empire the camp was rectangular, the length being about one-third greater than the breadth.

[2] § 68 (*d*). Distinguish *vallum* = 'palisade of stakes', *vallus* = 'stake'; but the latter is sometimes used in the sense of the former.

and the *porta decumana*, was reserved for the headquarters and the administrative part of the camp. Here, immediately behind the *via principalis* and at its central point, stood the general's

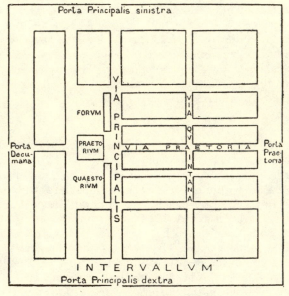

ROMAN CAMP

tent (*praetōrium*), with the *tribūnal* or earth-built platform from which he addressed his troops, and the *augurāle* where the omens were taken. Flanking the *praetorium* on one side was the *forum*, or soldiers' meeting-place, on the other the *quaestō-rium* or quarters of the quaestor. Between the inner area of the camp and the surrounding rampart there was a clear space 200 feet in breadth (*intervallum*), which served to protect the camp from hostile missiles and provided an exercise ground for the troops. In front of each gate there were usually on outpost duty (*in stătiōne*) one or two cohorts, while sentinels (*custōdes*) and pickets (*excŭbiae*) kept watch at the gates themselves or along the rampart. Night-guards (*vigiliae*) each consisted of four men, and were relieved four times between sunset and sunrise, so that *vigilia* (*prima, secunda*, &c.) came to denote a division of time. The watchword for the night was written on wooden tablets (*tessĕrae*), and distributed to the troops by four *tesserarii*, one from each legion.

A camp which was occupied for a considerable period (*castra stătīva*) was either *aestīva* ('summer camp') or *hīberna* ('winter'). The fortifications of the *stativa* were naturally more elaborate than those of the one-night bivouac, and in the case of the winter camp the soldiers were protected by regular barracks or huts (*căsae*) in place of the ordinary tents (*tentōria, pelles*).

§ 72. Sieges and Siege-Engines

The methods employed to capture a fortress were either (*a*) assault (*oppugnatio repentīna*), (*b*) investment (*obsĭdio*), or (*c*) a combination of investment and assault (*obsidio longinqua*).

(*a*) An assault was conducted by means of storming parties, who, after the trenches had been filled with fascines (*crātes*), broke down the gates or applied scaling-ladders (*scālae*) to the walls. Such parties were frequently protected, in approaching the walls, by the 'tortoise' (*testūdo*), an arrangement of locked shields, which the front rank held vertically and the ranks behind them horizontally.

(*b*) The investment was effected by a continuous line of entrenchments (*circumvallatio*), connecting a series of redoubts (*castella*), the object being to cut off the besieged from all supplies and starve them into surrender.

(*c*) Usually, however, the investment was only a preliminary to an organized system of attack (*oppugnatio*), the chief feature of which was the *agger*, a huge causeway of earth packed in a framework of beams or wattle-work built opposite a convenient point of the enemy's ramparts and gradually raised to an equal height with the latter. When the *agger* was finished, towers on wheels (*turres ambŭlātōriae*), of several stories (*tăbŭlāta*), were moved along it, or alongside it, close up to the walls;

artillery and light-armed troops operating from these could meet the besieged on equal, or superior, terms, and draw-bridges (*sambūcae*) could be let down on the ramparts.

While engaged on the earth-works, &c., the besiegers were protected from missiles by several kinds of contrivances:

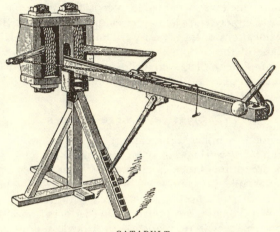

CATAPULT

wheeled screens (*plŭtĕi*), made of wicker-work covered with skins, or sheds (*vīnĕae*), varieties of which were the *muscŭli*, which protected sappers, and the *testūdines*, which covered parties working a ram (*ărĭes*). This last was a breaching instrument, consisting of a long iron-tipped beam suspended from a cross-bar, which was set in motion against the wall by its hinder end. There were also siege-hooks (*falces mūrāles*), poles with hooks at the end, for tearing out stones.

Roman artillery (*tormenta*), which was employed, as a rule, only in sieges, derived its power mainly from torsion, the various machines employed being, in principle, cross-bows of great size and strength.

The three chief kinds were the *cătăpulta*, the *ballista*, and the *scorpio*, of which the first and the third hurled arrows of varying weight, the second boulders or beams of wood.[1]

The counter-tactics of the besieged were the hurling of fire, blazing arrows (*phălārĭcae*), stones, &c.; endeavouring to smash the engines by dropping boulders, undermining the besiegers' towers, or checking their mines (*cŭnīcŭli*) by counter mines.

§ 73. Roman Triumph

A word may be said about the *triumph* (*trĭumphus*), which, during the republic, was the coveted distinction for every victorious Roman general. To qualify for a triumph, several conditions had to be satisfied: (*a*) the general must have commanded in person in the battle; (*b*) the battle must have been decisive; (*c*) at least 5,000 of the enemy, who must be foreign, must have been killed. If the senate was satisfied on these points, and decreed a triumph, a special vote was passed allowing the general to retain the full military *imperium* for the day within the city.

The triumphing general entered the city in a chariot drawn by four horses, wearing a laurel wreath, sceptre, crown, and a special robe (*tŏga picta*), which gave him the semblance of a king, if not of Jupiter himself. He was preceded by the captives and spoils taken in war and followed by his troops. The procession passed along the *Via Sacra* up to the temple of *Iuppiter Căpĭtōlīnus* on the Capitol, where sacrifice was offered.

A general who did not obtain a full triumph might be awarded a minor celebration (*ŏvatio*) or be honoured by a public thanksgiving lasting for so many days (*supplicatio*).

Under the empire a triumph, with very rare exceptions, was the prerogative of the emperor, all military successes being won under his auspices; a general now received instead, as a mark of honour, what were known as *triumphālia ornāmenta*, the right to wear triumphal dress at festivals.

----

§ 72.   [1] There is some confusion, however, in the use of these terms, which mean different things for different authorities.

§ 74. THE ROMAN NAVY

The Romans never concerned themselves much with maintaining an efficient naval force, and what interest they took in naval matters, at least under the republic, was forced upon them by the occasional circumstance of having an enemy who must be crushed at sea. It was in the long struggle with Carthage, notably the First Punic War,[1] that Rome may be said to have served her apprenticeship, and achieved her first success, as a sea-power; thereafter the chief occasions requiring sea operations were perhaps the suppression of the Cilician pirates by Pompey[2] and Octavian's (Augustus) struggle with Sex. Pompeius and Antony.[3] The creation of a permanent fleet was due to Augustus, who stationed squadrons at Misenum and Ravenna in Italy and at Forum Iulii (Fréjus) in Gallia Narbonensis for the defence of the Mediterranean; there was also an Egyptian squadron with its base at Alexandria, and flotillas guarded the Rhine and the Danube. Other provincial squadrons were created under the empire.

Ships of the fleet were either men-of-war (*naves longae*), mostly the same as the Greek trireme, or transports (*ŏnĕrāriae*). There were also lighter craft (e.g. *Liburnae*) used as dispatch-boats.

Crews were made up of oarsmen (*rēmĭges*), sailors (*nautae*), and marines (*prōpugnātōres, classiarii*). These, however, were not recruited from Roman citizens, but furnished almost entirely by the Italians, whence they came to be known as *socii nāvāles*. In imperial times, the crews were recruited mainly in the maritime provinces of the empire: the *classiarii* enlisted for twenty-six years and received the Roman citizenship on their discharge (*missio*). The emperor was head of all the fleets, and under him each was commanded by a *praefectus* whom he appointed, whilst the trading ships on the 'monsoon' route from Egypt to India sailed in convoy under imperial protection.

§ 74. [1] § 12. [2] § 33. [3] §§ 47–50.

ROMAN PRIVATE LIFE

§ 75. The Family

The keystone of the Roman state was the family (*fămĭlia*),[1] and the head of the family (*paterfamilias*) exercised, in the eye of the law, an almost despotic authority over the other members of it. This power over his children was his *patria potestas*, over his wife, *manus*; in respect of his slaves, he was *dominus* or absolute owner. All the property of the family belonged to the *paterfamilias* as the only recognized owner, and it was only of his grace that either son or slave was allowed to hold property of his own; this was in either case known as *pĕcūlium*. The *paterfamilias* might occasionally even inflict death on wife or son, as he might on a slave, though gradually the law interfered to protect the members of the family against the extreme rigour of the father's authority.

§ 76. Roman Names

Normally a Roman bore three names, called respectively *praenōmen*, *nōmen*, and *cognōmen*: e.g. *Gaius Iulius Caesar*. Of these, the *praenomen* was the personal or 'Christian' name; the *nomen*, which was the most important of the three, ended in *-ius*, and denoted the *gens* to which the person belonged (*nomen gentĭlĭcium*); the *cognomen* denoted the particular branch of the *gens* to which he belonged, and often had an obvious reference to some physical or mental peculiarity, e.g. *Capito, Naso, Calvus, Brutus*, &c. Other additional *cognomina*[1] might be derived from some exploit in the career of the bearer, e.g. the conquest of a country: cf. *Africānus, Măcĕdŏnĭcus, Crētĭcus*, &c.

In formal and official style, the father's, grandfather's, and even great-grandfather's names and the name of the individual's tribe were inserted between the *nomen* and *cognomen*:

---

§ 75.   [1] The word means 'the collection of *famuli*' (servants), and so signifies a man's whole household, not merely wife and children.

§ 76.   [1] Called in late Latin *agnomina*.

e.g. *M. Tullius M. f.* (i.e. *Marci filius*) *M. n.* (i.e. *Marci nepos*)
M. pr(onepos) Cor(nelia tribu) Cicero.

When a man passed by adoption into another family he
usually assumed all the names of his adopter, retaining as a
cognomen the name of his original *gens* with the addition of the
suffix *-ānus*: e.g. the son of L. Aemilius Paullus, the conqueror
of Macedonia,[2] when adopted by P. Cornelius Scipio became
P. Cornelius Scipio *Aemilianus.*

Women as a rule bore only the name of their *gens* in the
feminine: e.g. *Cornēlia, Līvia.* Slaves were originally designated
by a name ending in *-por* (an abbreviation of *puer*): e.g. *Marcipor,*
Lūcipor. When manumitted, they usually took their master's
nomen and *praenomen*, retaining their original name as *cognomen*:
e.g. Cicero's secretary became M. Tullius Tiro.

§ 77. Position of Women

Legally, the position of women may be described as one of
perpetual tutelage; in other words, the law directed that they
should always be in the power (*manus*) of fathers, brothers, or
husbands. The married woman, if she did not pass into the
manus of her husband, remained under that of her father; the
unmarried, on the death of her father, passed into that of her
nearest male relatives (*agnāti*). This stringent guardianship was
possibly designed to prevent the woman from disposing of the
family property at will. Though under these legal disabilities,[1]
the Roman matron enjoyed a much greater amount of freedom
in the ordering of her daily life than had been permitted among
the Greeks. As the honoured mistress of the household she was
addressed as *domina*; carried on her daily occupations[2] in the
main room (*ātrium*) of the house, and not, like her Greek sister,
in the seclusion of special apartments; and seems at all times to
have been at liberty to walk abroad and attend religious festivals

---

[2] § 19.

§ 77. [1] Later partly circumvented by the system of trusts (*fidei com-
missa*).

[2] Prominent among these was the preparation of wool for weaving:
lānifica as a term of commendation occurs frequently in epitaphs.

A ROMAN'S THREE NAMES in a Pompeian election placard of M(arcus)
Lucretius Fronto and C(aius) Lollius Fuscus

A MEDALLION OF THE FOURTH CENTURY showing a married couple;
the husband holds the marriage contract

Photograph Ashmolean Museum

THE SLAVE FREED. Relief dedicated by a freedman, Asclepiades (centre), who holds the hand of his wife, Arrania. On the left is his former master (patronus) C. H(elvius) Hermes

THE ROMAN AUCTION OF A SLAVE who stands in the centre with the auctioneer on one side and a bidder on the other. Relief on a sarcophagus from Capua

or banquets. In the period of the late republic and early empire there was an increasing disregard of the sanctity of the marriage tie, and perhaps some falling away in the morals of the women themselves; but even in the darkest days of the empire there were brilliant exceptions which challenged comparison with the noblest traditions of the family life of the republic.

§ 78. Slaves

Slavery was known at Rome from the earliest times, but the immense growth of the slave population was the direct result of the foreign conquests of Rome, which led to a great influx of the slave element from foreign countries.[1] Every household numbered its complement of slaves, who were employed in various capacities, not necessarily menial; for the slaves were often in many ways better educated than their masters, and acted as secretaries, copyists, librarians, and what not, or superintended the children's lessons. A large part of the manufacturing industry of Rome was, moreover, carried on by slaves. As a rule, the lot of the house-slave was much more tolerable than that of the gangs[2] who cultivated the large country estates of their owners, and it was accounted a punishment for a slave to be transferred from the town to the country. Roman law regarded the slave simply as a piece of property,[3] and the Roman master too often literally interpreted the law in the capriciousness and cruelty of his punishments, which might take the form of beating with the rod (*virga*), whip (*scŭtĭca, lōrum*), scourge (*flăgellum*), branding, or crucifixion. But slaves could purchase freedom with their savings (*peculium*) and, once manumitted, became full citizens. Manumission was in principle unrestricted and of frequent occurrence. Augustan laws checked irresponsible manumission. Under the empire, owing partly to the spread of Christianity, slaves enjoyed more humane treatment.

§ 78.   [1] Cf. the slave-names *Thrax, Syra,* &c.
[2] At night these were herded in a sort of barrack (*ergastulum*).
[3] *mancipium.*

§ 79. Marriage

Celibacy in the best days of the republic was looked upon with disfavour by the state, and was an object of censorial[1] displeasure. Under the empire marriage was directly encouraged by the conferring of special privileges on fathers of at least three children (*ius trium liberorum*).

There were several special forms of Roman marriage, according as the wife did or did not pass into the absolute power[2] (*manus*) of her husband. In the latter case the marriage depended on mere consent on the part of husband and wife, and did not involve any special ceremonies. In the former the union was effected in one or other of three ways: *confarreatio*, *coemptio*, and *ūsus*.

(*a*) The 'confarreate' marriage was a religious ceremony confined to patricians, and got its name from the cake of spelt (*far*) which was either eaten or offered at the ceremony.

(*b*) Marriage by *coemptio* was probably at first a plebeian ceremony, whereby the bride was figuratively sold to her husband in the presence of a scale-holder (*lībrĭpens*) and five witnesses.

(*c*) Marriage by *usus* depended on the wife spending a year with the husband, and not absenting herself from his house for more than three nights during that period.

Features common to all modes of marriage alike were (i) the betrothal (*sponsālia*), at which the man gave his fiancée a pledge (*arrha*), usually in the form of a ring; (ii) the actual ceremony, when the auspices were taken and the wedding contract (*tăbŭlae nuptiāles*) was signed. The bride wore a special dress (*tŭnĭca recta*), a flame-coloured veil (*flammeum*), and had her hair parted into six locks by a spear-shaped comb (*hasta caelĭbāris*). She was attended by a matron friend (*prōnŭba*). After prayer and sacrifice, the ceremony ended with the expression of good wishes by the guests, and a banquet (*cēna*) at the house of the bride's father; (iii) the *dēductio*, or escorting of the bride from her father's to the bridegroom's house, in a procession headed by

§ 79.   [1] § 55 (censor).   [2] § 77.

BIRTH AND CHILDHOOD; from a relief partly restored in the Louvre

Photograph Giraudon

A PROFESSOR'S CLASSROOM. From a sarcophagus in Berlin

MOSAIC from the Roman villa at Low Ham, Somerset. It illustrates Virgil's story of Dido and Aeneas. (Now in Taunton Museum)

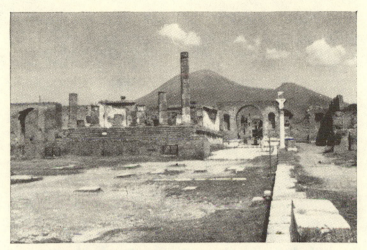

THE FORUM AT POMPEII, with Vesuvius in the distance

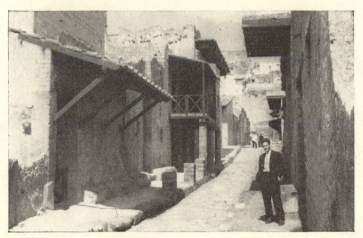

A STREET IN HERCULANEUM

Photographs Barri-Jones

torch-bearers and flute-players, and usually accompanied by a considerable crowd of people. On the evening of the following day a banquet (*rĕpōtia*) was given at the bridegroom's house.

§ 80. Birth and Childhood

The phrase *tollere* or *suscipere lĭberos* probably preserves the symbolic act whereby the father lifted the newly born child from the ground in token of his intention to rear it. For he was not bound to do so, and the exposure of female or deformed infants was not uncommon, though both law and humanity combined to mitigate the practice. On the ninth day after birth the child was solemnly purified (*dies lustricus*), and probably received its *praenomen*. Now, too, the free-born child (*ingĕnŭus*) had suspended from its neck the *bulla* or amulet, which was of gold, if the parents were well off, and of leather (or bronze) if they were poor. It was worn by boys till the assumption of the *tŏga vĭrīlis* (16–17), and by girls probably till marriage.

§ 81. Education

Children at first were trained at home by their mothers; boys when they grew older attended their fathers about their ordinary occupations, and so learned their future duties. Parental instruction in whatever form was mainly directed to inculcating the elementary Roman virtues of thrift and industry and respect for ancestral custom (*mos maiōrum*) rather than to mere book-knowledge. But schools were in existence at a comparatively early date, and by the first century B.C. a regular educational course, largely influenced by Greek models, had been established, in which three stages may be distinguished: (*a*) the elementary school (*lūdus*) presided over by the *litterător* or *ludi magister*, who taught 'the three R's'; (*b*) the school of the *grammăticus*, where attention was given to the expounding of the Greek poets, notably Homer, and afterwards of Latin poets as well; (*c*) the school of the *rhētor* or teacher of rhetoric, whose pupils were exercised in composition and declamation. The training under the *rhetor* was highly elaborated in imperial times and was considered the crown of Roman education. It may thus be said that the education of the Roman boy was governed from the outset by the single aim of making him an effective public speaker. Towards the end of the republic young Romans often went abroad for a course of rhetoric and philosophy, especially at Athens, which was in a sense the university of the Roman world. Cicero and Horace, e.g., both studied at Athens.

A Roman boy began to attend school about the age of seven, and boys and girls were probably taught together, though this is not certain. The children of the wealthy classes, at least, were attended to and from school by a slave called by the Greek name *paedăgōgus*, who also to some extent supervised their conduct and studies. Sometimes another slave (*capsārius*) might be employed to carry the child's books. School began early in the morning, and discipline was strict; punishment was administered with the cane (*fĕrŭla*) or the *scŭtĭca*. There were two regular school holidays in the year: one in December at the time of the *Sāturnālia*, and one at the *Quinquātrūs*, a festival of Minerva (19–25 March), at which latter time the yearly fees appear to have been paid.

§ 82. The Roman House

The chief, and originally perhaps the only, room of the ordinary Roman house (*domus*) was the *ātrium*, an oblong apartment with a roof sloping inwards and downwards so as to leave a rectangular opening (*complŭvium*), immediately beneath which was a basin of similar form (*implŭvium*) sunk in the floor to catch the rain-water which entered by the *compluvium*. The *atrium* was originally the living room of the family. Gradually a series of smaller rooms were built round the *atrium*, these being used as sleeping-chambers (*cŭbĭcŭla*), store-rooms (*cellae*), and the like. At either end of the *atrium* there was an open recess (*āla*), where, in the case of distinguished families, the portrait-masks (*imāgines*) of ancestors were kept. Between the *atrium* and the street there was usually a corridor (*vestĭbŭlum*), closed at a certain point by

THE TOILET OF A ROMAN LADY. One slave holds the mirror while another dresses her mistress's hair

Photograph Landesmuseum, Trier

the *iānŭa* which consisted of two heavy folding doors (*valvae*), opening inwards. The rooms on either side of the entrance corridor were generally let as shops (*tăbernae*).

Opening out of the *atrium* and separated from it only by a curtain, if at all, was the *tablīnum*, used perhaps mostly as a reception room, with dining-rooms on either side.

Behind the *tablīnum*, and connected with it by a side passage (*andrōn*), was the *peristyle* (*peristўlium*), which was really a garden with pillars on two, three, or four sides, and had usually a separate entrance (*postīcum*) from a side street. The peristyle was occasionally flanked by bedrooms. Larger houses might have a second peristyle and a garden beyond. The peristyle, as was natural from its greater privacy and ampler space, gradually superseded the *atrium* as the living room, the latter being then used mostly as a reception room.

Meals were originally served in the *atrium*; after the practice of reclining at meals was firmly established, special dining-rooms with three couches (*trīclīnia*) were built in the peristyle.

Outwardly, the ordinary Roman house must have been bare and unpretentious, partly from its lowness (a second story was not common), and from the smallness and fewness of its windows; inside it usually presented a much more magnificent appearance with its floors of mosaic and wall-paintings.

From the *domus* or private dwelling-house must be distinguished (*a*) the *insulae*[1] or large tenement houses of several stories let out in flats to several families of the poorer class, and (*b*) the *villae* or country-houses of the wealthy. The latter, while preserving the essential features of the town residence, were as a rule more irregular, covered more ground, and were generally on a more elaborate scale.

§ 83. Roman Dress

The proper and ordinary dress of the Roman citizen was the *tŏga*—the distinctive national garb. In its normal form, this was a large piece of white woollen stuff shaped like the segment of

§ 82.   [1] Lit. 'islands'—so called from being surrounded by streets on all sides.

a circle, and measuring about eighteen feet along the straight edge with a depth of about seven. In putting on, the toga was first thrown over the left shoulder, the curved edge covering the left arm, and about one-third of the total length falling free in front towards the feet. The remaining two-thirds was then carried round the back and under the right arm, after which it was gathered in a mass of folds, resembling a belt (*balteus*), and thrown over the left shoulder. In this process, however, about one-third of the depth was allowed to fall over to the front: this formed a series of folds (*sinus*) reaching to the knee. The adjustment was completed by next pulling up a portion of the part which first of all dropped from the left shoulder to the ground, the portion so drawn up being arranged in a 'boss' (*umbo*) of folds over the *balteus* at the waist. The toga, properly adjusted, formed a singularly graceful dress; but being somewhat heavy and cumbrous, as well as difficult to keep clean, it gradually ceased to be worn except on formal occasions.

A special toga with a purple hem (*toga praetexta*) was worn by free-born boys and girls, the former exchanging it at their sixteenth birthday for the 'gown of manhood' (*toga virīlis*)—an event of some importance in a boy's life. A *toga praetexta* was worn also by the curule magistrates and the higher orders of priests. Candidates for office had their toga specially whitened with chalk (*crētāta*).

Under the toga was worn the *tŭnĭca*, a sort of shirt with short sleeves, reaching a little way below the knees, and often girded with a belt (*cingŭlum*). Under the *tunica* again there was frequently worn a close-fitting vest (*sŭbūcŭla*). Other upper garments worn from time to time were the *paenŭla*, a close-fitting sleeveless cloak of coarse material, used in wet weather or on journeys, and the *lăcerna*, a more open cloak, generally fastened on the right shoulder with a brooch (*fĭbŭla*).

The distinctive dress of the Roman matron was the *stŏla*—a long tunic reaching to the feet, with short sleeves, and showing a narrow border (*instĭta*) at the bottom. A girdle was worn over it at the waist, and underneath it a *subucula*. The *stola* was the ordinary indoor garment; out of doors an over-wrap (*palla*)

End of the second century and early third century

A Roman Lady of the early empire. Naples Museum

FASHIONS IN HAIRDRESSING

was worn, a large piece of woollen stuff which might be adjusted in a variety of ways, but normally was arranged somewhat after the style of the toga. Girls and foreign women wore a tunic and palla.

The Romans, as a rule, went bare-headed, but on occasion they wore a broad-brimmed hat (*pětăsus*) to keep off the sun; the *pilleus* or felt cap was used by those who were much exposed to the weather, and was also a mark of newly acquired freedom.

Foot-wear consisted of *calcei*, shoes covering the whole feet, or *sŏlěae*, sandals. *Calcei* were of different kinds, according to the rank of the wearer, the most important varieties being the *calceus senātōrius*, with an ivory crescent (*lūnŭla*) in front, and the red *mulleus* worn by patrician magistrates. Indoors, and when dining out, it was the custom to wear sandals (*soleae*). The *cǎlǐga*, a heavy hob-nailed boot, was worn chiefly by soldiers and peasants.

§ 84. A Roman Day: Occupations, Meals, &c.

The Roman day, for all ordinary purposes, was reckoned as the period between sunrise and sunset, which was divided into twelve hours (*hōrae*). It follows that a Roman 'hour' was of varying length according to the season of the year. At mid-winter it would be about three-quarters of a modern hour in length, at midsummer just over an hour and a quarter. The night was correspondingly divided into four watches (*vǐgǐlǐae*) of three hours each,[1] and further into somewhat vaguer sections, such as 'lamp-lighting' (*prima fax*), 'bed-time' (*concǔbia*), 'cock-crow' (*gallǐcǐnǐum*), &c.

Business in the morning, rest and recreation in the afternoon, may be described as the ordinary Roman practice. A representative Roman would be occupied the first two hours of the day (about 7–9) with receiving morning callers (*sǎlūtatio*). This was a special feature of Roman life in imperial times, when the rich man's callers received their dole (*sportǔla*).[2] Thereafter

---

§ 84. [1] § 71.
[2] First of food, afterwards converted into an equivalent in money.

came the serious business of the day, which might be of various character: the third hour (9–10) was especially devoted to the business of the law-courts, and other duties which might claim attention were attendance at certain legal ceremonies (witnessing wills, betrothals, assumption of the *toga virīlis*, &c.), complimentary visits, and the like.

The first meal of the day was the *ientāculum* or light breakfast. At the sixth hour (twelve o'clock) the *prandium* or light midday meal was taken, and this was followed by a short siesta (*merī-diatio*). The interval between the siesta and dinner-time was devoted to exercise, either in the *Campus Martius* or at the *palaestrae* of the baths, where the young and vigorous might indulge in running, jumping, wrestling, and other forms of athletics: older men might have a game of ball (*trĭgōn*), always a popular Roman pastime. Exercise of whatever kind was usually regarded as a preliminary to the bath, which played a great part in Roman life, especially under the empire, when great public baths (*thermae*) such as those of Trajan and Caracalla were erected. The Roman full-course bath was a very elaborate process, corresponding somewhat to the Turkish bath of modern times.

After the bath came the chief meal of the day—dinner (*cēna*)—at the ninth hour (i.e. 3–4 p.m.) The *cena* was, or might be, an elaborate and lengthy repast, three hours being considered a moderate time to devote to it. It consisted of three parts: (*a*) the *gustus* (otherwise *gustatio* or *prōmulsis*); (*b*) the *cena* proper, in several courses (*fercŭla*); (*c*) the *mensae secundae* or dessert. The normal number of a dinner-party was nine, who were accommodated on couches surrounding three sides of the table, the open side enabling the servants to hand the food. The couches (*lecti*) were known as *summus*, *medius*, and *īmus*, according to their respective dignity. An invited guest might occasionally bring another with him, who was known as his 'shadow' (*umbra*). The guests, after removing their sandals (*soleae*), reclined on their left elbow, which rested on a cushion. Knives and forks not being in use, napkins (*mappae*) were much more necessary than nowadays for the guests to wipe their fingers

with. During the meal the guests might be entertained with
music and singing. The *cena* was frequently followed by a drink-
ing bout (*cōmissatio*), at which one of the guests was chosen
magister or *arbiter bibendi*, his function being to regulate the pro-
portions in which the wine and water were to be mixed, for wine
was practically never drunk neat. The best wines came from
Campania, the Caecuban, Setine, Falernian, and Massic being
well-known brands.

After dark the street conditions at Rome were not inviting:
there seems to have been no systematic method of lighting, and
danger was to be apprehended from heavy traffic which was not
allowed to pass during the day, as well as from roving bands of
young nobles similar to the London Mohocks of the early
eighteenth century.

§ 85. Amusements

Roman amusements may be considered under the heads of
(*a*) public, (*b*) private. The public amusements, during the
republic, may be described as adjuncts of some of the great
religious festivals, e.g. the *Ludi Romani* in honour of Jupiter, *Ludi
Apollinārēs, Ludi Megalenses*,[1] &c. By the end of the republican
period such regular festivals had come to claim no less than
seventy-six days of the year, and this period was often added
to by extraordinary games, e.g. *ludi prīvāti*, organized and
managed by individuals. *Ludi* in a more special sense may be
distinguished as (*a*) *ludi scaenici*, performances in the theatre,
consisting mostly of tragedies and comedies adapted from the
Greek, (*b*) *ludi circenses* or games of the circus, which had a great
hold on the populace under the empire. The second class comprised (i) the chariot races in the circus, (ii) gladiatorial displays
(*mūnera*), and (iii) beast-baitings (*vēnationes*), at which last
enormous numbers of animals were sometimes slaughtered,
e.g. 11,000 in celebration of Trajan's victory over the Dacians.

The private amusements of Roman society were not usually
of an intellectual order. Playing with dice for a stake was one

§ 85.   [1] In honour of the *Magna Mater* or mother of the gods.

of the commonest. Dice were of two kinds: *tessĕrae* or cubes, marked on each of their six sides with numbers from one to six, and thrown out of a box (*phīmus*, *frĭtillus*): the other kind, *tāli*

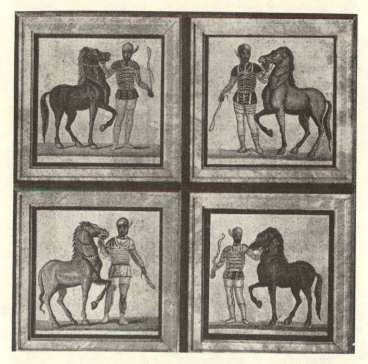

CHARIOT DRIVERS AND THEIR HORSES. Each has a distinctive coloured uniform and a 'crash-helmet'
Photograph Bradford

(lit. 'knuckle-bones'), were marked on four sides with the numbers 1, 3, 4, 6. In playing, four *tali* were used, the highest cast being known as the *Vĕnus*, the lowest as the *cănis*. Another common game was that known as *mĭcare digitis* ('odd and even'), in which one party quickly opened a number of his fingers and the other guessed the number.

§ 86. A Roman Funeral

When a Roman died arrangements for the funeral were made with professional undertakers (*lĭbĭtīnarii*), who had their head-quarters at the temple of *Venus Lĭbĭtīna*. The deceased was laid out (*collŏcatio*) in the *atrium* of the house, with his feet turned towards the door. Before the house was placed a branch of pine or cypress to warn passers-by against pollution. In the case of a distinguished personage whose funeral was public (*fūnus indictīvum*),[1] the people were summoned to attend by a crier (*praeco*) in a set form of words. The procession was marshalled by a *dissignātor*, and comprised musicians (*cornĭcines, tībīcines*), hired mourners (*praefĭcae*), sometimes also a mummer (*mīmus*) who imitated the gestures of the dead, and—what must have been a striking feature—a train of men wearing the portrait-masks (*ĭmāgines*) of the deceased's ancestors who had held curule office. The train passed on to the *forum*, where the bier was deposited in front of the *rostra*. Here a panegyric (*laudatio*) was pronounced over the deceased, while the figures of his ancestors formed a half-circle around him. Thereafter the pro-cession went its way to the family burying-ground outside the walls, where the corpse was burned on a pyre (*rŏgus*), after which the ashes were collected and placed in an urn (*olla, urna*). The last farewell (*vale*) was uttered, and the mourners returned. A period of nine days' mourning followed, ending with an offering of food (*sacrĭfĭcium nŏvendĭāle*) at the tomb. From the middle of the fifth century B.C. cremation was com-moner than inhumation, except in the case of certain families, e.g. the Cornelii.

§ 87. THE ROMAN CHARACTER

The Romans were never a distinct race. After 89 B.C. all citi-zens of Italian towns were *cives Romani*, i.e. Romans. In suc-ceeding centuries both the citizen body as a whole and the governing class came to consist of members of all nations and

---

§ 86.   [1] An ordinary funeral was *funus translātīcium*.

races included within the empire. But the *prisca virtus* (primitive excellence) attributed to Romans of the early Republic continued to have potency as an ideal after the reality had faded. To the Romans, the word that expressed the Roman national character was *grăvitas*, which denotes a certain seriousness of

THE COLOSSEUM IN ROME. Enlarged and finished in A.D. 80 by the Emperor Titus. The arena was 206 × 170 yards, and there were seats for 45,000 spectators
Photograph Mansell

thought and purpose and reserve of manner—the qualities which give a man *weight* or *dignity*. Corresponding to this general term, or as elements included in it, may be noticed: (*a*) the Roman respect for, and obedience to, duly constituted authority in whatever form, whether that of a properly elected magistrate, or of a general in the field, or of the head of the family (*patria potestas*),[1] or of ancestral custom (*mos maiōrum*); (*b*) the high ideal of the purity of family life and the honour accorded to women; (*c*) dutiful affection towards parents and country (*pĭĕtas*).

§ 87.   [1] § 75.

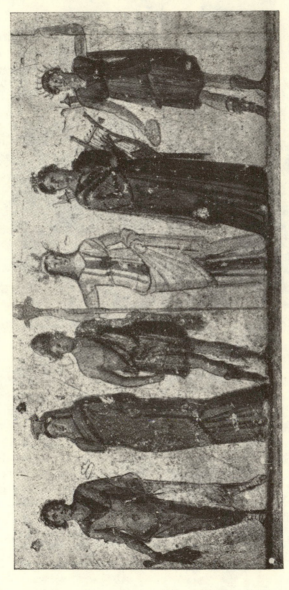

A GROUP OF ROMAN GODS from a wall-painting at Pompeii. From left to right Mercury, Isis, Castor, Vesta, Apollo, and Diana

These were some of the qualities which made the Romans great—qualities, on the whole, which inspire respect rather than affection; and it may be added that, combined with these, was a certain hardness and lack of sympathy with such aesthetic and intellectual pursuits as had distinguished the Greeks. This trait in the Roman character is reflected to a certain extent in the fascination which the cruel sports of the amphitheatre possessed for the Roman populace.

§ 88. ROMAN RELIGION

The basis of the Roman's religion was the primitive conception of the existence of certain unseen powers which influenced for good or evil the minutest details and operations of his daily life. These powers gradually received appropriate titles indicative of the special sphere in which their influence was manifested: thus there was the god (or spirit) of sowing (*Sāturnus*), the spirit of the woods (*Silvānus*), the spirit of boundaries (*Termĭnus*), and so on. Such powers required to be placated in order to avert their malign influence, and they had to be placated in the proper way: hence arose set forms of ritual and the need of proper functionaries to carry out such ritual with the necessary exactness. If this was done—if the Roman, one might say, fulfilled his part of the contract—he expected the power concerned to fulfil his in the way of protecting his flocks, crops, or what not. It should be observed, further, that these unseen powers never had for the Roman the same definitely conceived personality that they had for the Greek: they were at best more or less colourless abstractions (*nūmina*). Hence the Roman religion was a rather cold and formal thing, containing little of the moral or spiritual element which we associate with the word. And yet the idea of living under obligations to superior powers, which is perhaps the true meaning of the word *rĕlĭgio* (*rĕlĭgare* = 'bind', and so 'bounden duty') was not without its effect in the upbuilding of the Roman character and in conducing to the strength and stability of the Roman state.

§ 89. Roman Gods

Of the divinities who, amid the multitudinous supernatural powers endowed with a special function (*nūmina*), were elevated to a level more or less corresponding to that of the members of the Greek Pantheon, two of the earliest and most characteristic, inherited from the Romans' Aryan ancestors, were *Iuppiter*, the god of the bright sky, and *Vesta*, the goddess of the hearth and home, and the centre of the Roman family religion. Jupiter was worshipped under many names denoting the various ways in which he manifested his power: as *Iuppiter Feretrius* (perhaps = 'the striker') he was presented with the *spolia ŏpīma* by the general who had slain in battle the general of the enemy; as *Iuppiter Stător* he was the god who stayed flight in battle, or maybe gave endurance to the state. Under the later and most honoured of all his titles, *Optimus Maximus*, his temple on the Capitol was the distinctive centre of the national religious life. The importance of Vesta will be readily appreciated when it is remembered how large a place the family and its rites occupied in Roman life, and how high was the respect paid to the Vestal Virgins, her priestesses.

Other distinctively Italian deities were *Mars* or *Māvors*, the god of growth and creative power, and of 'manliness', especially as exhibited in war, with which he was prominently associated; *Quĭrīnus*, a Sabine deity resembling Mars, worshipped on the Quirinal; *Sāturnus*, the ancient god of sowing; *Cĕres*, the goddess of fertility and crops; *Păles* and *Faunus*, the guardians of flocks; *Iūno*, the special deity of women, with many attributes; *Mĭnerva*, the goddess of wisdom; *Vĕnus*, the goddess of love and grace; *Iānus*, the two-faced god of opening and shutting, and *Diăna*, the moon-goddess of many names; *Neptūnus*, the god of water.

There was a growing tendency among the Romans, especially those who read Greek literature or imitated Greek literary models, to identify some of their gods with Greek gods who had similar names or functions (thus Mars was identified with Ărēs, Neptunus with Pŏseidōn), and even to import new deities altogether. The Romans as a rule were very tolerant in the

A ROMAN RELIEF of priests and priestesses of Isis in procession with the instruments of the cult

matter of introducing foreign divinities, and from the time of the Second Punic War this process went on apace, oriental and especially Egyptian cults, such as the worship of *Īsis* and *Ŏsīris*, being very popular.

Some mention must be made of a prominent feature of Roman religion, which was of great influence in the family life —the worship, or something very much akin, accorded to the *Di Mānes*, or spirits of the departed, which, if neglected, became evil, mischievous ghosts (*Larvae, Lĕmŭres*). The *Lăres*, originally deities of the farm-land, were also worshipped at the crossways, but their most important cult was in association with that of the *Pĕnātes* (guardians of the family larder, *penus*) and with the worship of Vesta within the Roman family. The supervision of this worship was in the hands of the *paterfamilias*, and constituted an important element in his high authority.[1]

§ 90. Temples and Priests

The word *templum* means properly a space marked off for sacred purposes, and might be used of any place set apart by the *augur* for making his observations or of the part of the sky selected by him for the taking of omens. In a more restricted sense, it meant a building dedicated to a god, which in its simplest form consisted of nothing more than a *cella* or chamber to contain the image of the deity, before which stood an altar (*āra*). In course of time, elaborate buildings were erected as temples, but these were not used as places of worship, and were in fact often used for secular purposes.

The priests at Rome did not form a separate class, and no special training was required for their duties: the chief priesthoods in fact were usually filled by men who had distinguished themselves as statesmen or generals—a striking indication of the extent to which religion and the state were identified.

Two classes of priests may be distinguished: (*a*) those who were charged with a general supervision of the state religion, (*b*) the priests of particular deities. Of the first class there were

§ 89.   [1] § 75.

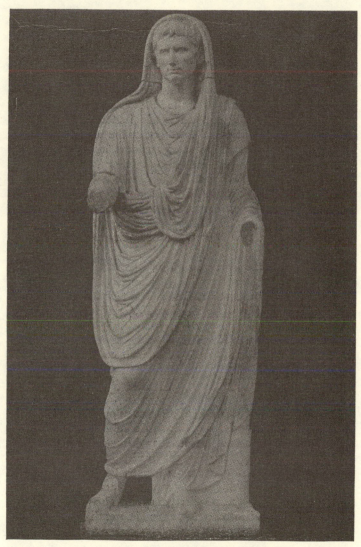

AUGUSTUS, sacrificing as Pontifex Maximus

I

two great colleges (*collēgia*)—the Pontiffs and the Augurs. The *Pontĭfĭces*, as their name implies, seem to have had originally as their special function the superintendence of the bridges (or roads) of the state; in historical times their control extended to all matters connected with religion, including the regulation of the calendar. Chief of their number, which was raised to fifteen under the republic, was the *Pontifex Maximus*, the official head of the Roman religion. Next in importance came the *Augurs*, whose duty it was to ascertain the will of the gods regarding any contemplated state business. In this they were guided by omens drawn from the flight or cries of birds in accordance with a fixed set of rules, which constituted the science (*disciplīna*) of augury. From the augurs must be distinguished the *hăruspĭces* or diviners from Etruria, who inspected the entrails of victims offered in sacrifice, interpreted the meaning of lightnings, &c., but these were not accounted so honourable as the augurs.

Of the priests of special divinities the most important were the three *Flāmĭnes* ('kindlers') of Jupiter (*Flamen Dĭālis*), Mars, and Quĭrīnus); the twelve Arval Brothers (*Fratres Arvāles*), whose hymn for seed-time invoked Mars (*Marmor*) and the *Lăres Consītīvi* (gods of sowing); the *Salii* ('leaping priests' of Mars'); and the six *Vestal Virgins* who kept the sacred fire ever alight in the temple of Vesta, the common hearth of the city.

§ 91. Ritual of Worship

The ritual of worship among the Romans consisted of prayer and sacrifice, the two being always combined. The victim (*victĭma, hostia*), after being sprinkled with wine and fragments of the sacred cake (*mŏla salsa*), was slain by the priest's assistant (*pŏpa*). The internal organs and especially the liver were carefully examined, and if of good omen were placed upon the altar (*porrectio*): the rest of the animal was eaten. The priest repeated a prayer with veiled head and under his breath, while a piper (*tībīcen*) played to drown all ill-omened sounds, the bystanders meanwhile maintaining a strict silence (*făvēre linguis*). To obtain the desired result, that is, the beneficent action of the deity within the sphere of his special activity, in a material sense—for there is little trace in the Roman religion of prayer for other

PRIEST OF CYBELE holding in his right hand the holy water sprinkler, in his left a basket of fruit. Round him are tympana, a scourge, and the mystic chest which held the holiest things of the ritual

than material blessings—every detail of the ritual had to be gone through with minute care: any mistake or accidental hindrance made it necessary to begin the whole process over again (*instaurare*), and to offer an expiatory sacrifice (*piăcŭlum*).

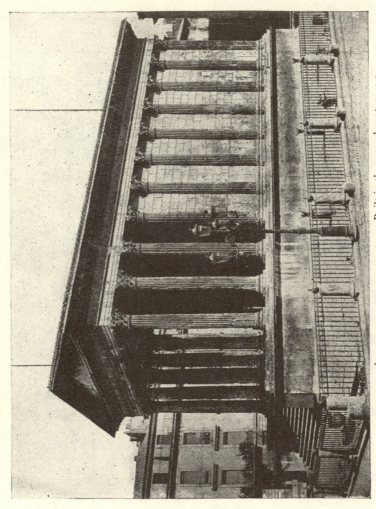

TEMPLE AT NÎMES IN SOUTHERN FRANCE. Built in the second century A.D.
Photograph Mansell

§ 92. ROMAN MONEY

The word *pĕcūnia* points to the primitive custom of reckoning value in cattle (*pecus*). Although Greek cities in S. Italy were coining from the sixth century onwards and Etruscans from *c.* 450, the Romans continued to be satisfied with barter or the use of copper weighed in the balance (*aes rŭde*) or, later, stamped bars of bronze (*aes signātum*). In 269 for the first time the Romans issued stamped coins, both silver and bronze, along with cast bronze coins (*aes grăve*) consisting of the unit *as* and fractions and multiples of it. These coins were issued from Rome and three other Italian mints, each of which had its own coin-types, and were intended to serve the monetary needs of Roman Italy. The strain of warfare, especially in the Second Punic War, led to successive reductions in weight and value of the *as*, but in *c.* 187 a new start was made with the first issue of the silver *dēnārius*, equated with 10 (reduced) *asses*, along with fractional coins, the *quīnārius* (= 5 *asses*) and the *sestertius* (= 2½ *asses*).[1] The *denarius* (= 4 *sestertii*) would equal about 10*d.* of our money.

The *sestertius* was seldom coined owing to its inconvenient smallness;[2] the *denarius* was the silver coin in ordinary use and continued to be so throughout the early Empire. But the *sestertius* was the ordinary unit of reckoning even for the largest sums (cf. the *franc* or *rupee* in modern times). Different sums were expressed in different ways:

(i) Sums under 2,000 sesterces were expressed by the cardinal numbers: e.g. *centum sestertii, ducenti sestertii,* &c.

(ii) Sums of 2,000 sesterces and upwards (acc. to the use of *mīlia*) would be represented as so many *milia sestertium,* e.g. *tria milia sestertium,* where *sestertium* is the older form of the gen. plur. of *sestertius*: this came to be treated as a neut. sing = 1,000

§ 92.　[1] Hence the symbol for this coin, HS—a corruption of IIS, i.e. 2½ (S = sēmis). The sestertius was also called *nummus*.

[2] The sestertius of the Empire was a larger coin, of yellow bronze (*orichalcum*).

sesterces, and hence arose the expression *trina*[3] *sestertia* = *tria milia sestertium*.

(iii) Millions of sesterces were expressed by a numeral adverb with *centēna milia sestertium* (*sestertium* again being gen. plur.): thus 2,000,000 sesterces = *vīcies centena milia sestertium*. Often

SHOPS IN THE FORUM OF TRAJAN
built early in the second century
Photograph Bradford

the *centena milia* was omitted, so that *vicies sestertium* or even *vicies* alone represents 'twenty times (a hundred thousand) sesterces', and *sestertium* being treated as a neuter noun is found in the gen. and abl. sing.

N.B.—A million sesterces (*decies sestertium* = 1,000,000 *sestertii*) was about £10,000.

Gold was rarely coined at Rome until the conquest of the East brought a great influx of wealth into the capital: the *aureus* of Julius Caesar was worth 25 *denarii* or 100 sesterces.

Interest was reckoned at first by fractions of the capital, the

---

[3] The distributive numeral was commonly used.

as being taken as the unit for this purpose; thus under the Decemvirs the legal rate was *fēnus unciārium* or $\frac{1}{12}$ of the capital, being $8\frac{1}{3}$ per cent. for a year of 10 months, and equivalent to 10 per cent. for a year of 12 months. This, about the middle of the fourth century B.C., was reduced to *sēmunciārium fenus* or $\frac{1}{24}$ of the capital = 5 per cent. From the time of Sulla interest was usually reckoned by the month, the legal rate being fixed at $\frac{1}{100}$ of the capital per month (*centēsima*) or 12 per cent. per annum.

§ 93. THE ROMAN CALENDAR

The Romans divided time into years and months, as we do: the division into weeks was not in use before the introduction of Christianity. The normal year which, prior to the time of Julius Caesar, extended to 355 days, was divided into twelve (apparently lunar) months, starting with March and ending with February, and called by the names which we have taken over from the Romans. The months *Iulius* and *Augustus*, which were originally known as *Quintīlis* (the fifth) and *Sextīlis* (the sixth) respectively, were so called in honour of Julius Caesar and Augustus.

In this lunar year of 355 days, March, May, July, and October had each 31 days; February had 28, and each of the other months 29. In order to bring this short year into agreement with the solar year of 365 days, a period of 22 or 23 days was intercalated (*mensis intercālāris*) in alternate years, after February 23, the rest of this month being omitted.

The whole arrangement of the calendar was in the hands of the Pontiffs,[1] who, for political purposes, might curtail or extend the year. By the time of Julius Caesar's dictatorship the confusion had become so great, from the omission of intercalation and other causes, that the year was two months in advance of the seasons. To remedy this Caesar enacted that the year 46 B.C. should consist of 445 days. The reformed or Julian

§ 93. [1] § 90.

Calendar was introduced on the 1st of January, 45 B.C. According to it, the number of days in each month was made what it now is, bringing the year up to 365 days instead of 355: every four years an extra day was to be added, between the 23rd and 24th of February. As the 24th of February was the sixth day before the Calends of March, the inserted day came to be known as *bissextus* ('twice sixth'): hence the year which contains this day is sometimes spoken of as 'bissextile'. The average length of the Julian year was thus 365¼ days, which was near enough the truth to cause no serious inconvenience till the Gregorian system corrected the slight error that remained.

§ 94. Method of Dating

In each month the Romans distinguished three main days, determined no doubt by the phases of the moon: these were (*a*) the Calends (*Kălendae*), the first day of the month, so called from the custom of the pontiff in early times to proclaim (*cǎlare*) its advent to the people, (*b*) the Nones (*Nōnae*) which fell on the fifth, and (*c*) the Ides (*Īdūs*) which fell on the thirteenth, except in March, May, July, and October (all long months) when the Nones fell on the 7th and the Ides on the 15th. In denoting the remaining days, to which no special name was given, the Romans looked forward to the next succeeding day which had a designation of its own, and then reckoned backwards, counting, however, the day from which they reckoned: thus, e.g., the 4th of March was called the 4th day before the Nones, the 13th of March was the 3rd day before the Ides, and so on. A day *after* the Ides was designated as so many days *before the Calends of the following month*.

Thus the readiest way of reckoning a day is (i) for a date between the Calends and Nones, or between the Nones and Ides, to subtract the number of the day mentioned from the number of the day on which the Nones or Ides fall, and add *one* (for the inclusive reckoning); (ii) for a date between the Ides and the Calends, to subtract the number of the day mentioned from the number of the days in the month, and add *two* (i.e. one for the inclusive reckoning, and one because the Calends are not the last of the month in which the date lies, but the first of the following month).

Note, however, that the day immediately preceding any of the three chief days is *pridie*, followed by the day in question in the accusative case: e.g. the 4th of January is *pridie Nonas Ianuarias*, the 31st of December is *pridie Kalendas Ianuarias*.

The common abbreviation by which the 10th of April, for instance, was expressed as *a. d. iv. Id. Apr.* (i.e. *ante diem quartum Idus Apriles*) seems to have arisen as follows: the original expression was 'before (on the fourth day) the Ides of April', the exact day being thrown in parenthetically in the ablative and then attracted into the accusative owing to the *ante* preceding. This abbreviated expression was considered as a single word, and might itself depend on a preposition: e.g. *differre aliquid in ante diem xv. Kal. Nov.*, 'to put off something to the 18th October'.

A particular year was usually designated by the names of the consuls for that year, e.g. *L. Pisone, A. Gabinio consulibus* is the year 58 B.C. But it might also be reckoned 'from the founding of the city' (*ab urbe condita, A.U.C.*), the beginning of the Roman era, which tradition made correspond with the year 753 B.C. To convert a year B.C. into a year A.U.C., subtract it from 754 (adding one for the Roman inclusive reckoning): e.g. 60 B.C. will be A.U.C. 694. To convert a year A.D. into a year A.U.C., add it to 753, e.g. A.D. 14 will be A.U.C. 767.

§ 95. THE LATIN LANGUAGE

Latin was the language spoken by the inhabitants of Latium, a comparatively small district on the western side of Italy, of which Rome was the chief city. Rome by her conquests spread her language over the neighbouring countries, with the result that the languages of modern Italy, France, Spain, Portugal and certain other districts claim Latin as their parent. The Latin, however, which developed into the so-called *Romance* languages was the colloquial or vulgar Latin that was used in everyday life: this was natural, as the Roman element in the provinces was represented mainly by soldiers and traders.

This popular Latin, of which our knowledge is but scanty, differed materially from the standard literary language which has been preserved to us by Roman authors, and which we read and try to write. It is this latter, the classical Latin of literature, that we understand for all ordinary purposes when we speak of 'Latin'.

After the breaking up of the Western Roman Empire in the fifth century of our era, the Church became the depositary of the traditions of Latin learning, and Latin revived as a literary language in the hands of ecclesiastical writers, not without, as was to be expected, some loss of purity, for the 'classical' period was now left far behind. The 'revival of learning' in the fourteenth century was the means of bringing classical Latin once more into prominence as the medium of international and learned intercourse, and this it continued to be in the centuries immediately following,[1] and continues still, to some extent, even in our own day, as the recognized universal language of science and philosophy.

When we consider the numerous points at which modern western civilization touches that of Rome, or indeed, one might say, the extent to which its character has been determined by the latter—the fact that Roman law is the basis of the legal systems of the most highly civilized nations of modern times, and that the Latin language, besides being the parent of the Romance languages of western Europe, has contributed so largely, directly or indirectly, to the making of the English language—it is obvious that a knowledge of Latin and of Latin literature is not merely a necessity for the student of modern European literature, but constitutes an indispensable element in a liberal education.

§ 96. ROMAN LITERATURE

It was only after Rome in the course of her conquest of Italy had been brought into contact with the cities of Magna Graecia in the south that anything in the shape of an artistic Roman literature arose. It is true that before this epoch there existed

§ 95.   [1] Thus Milton was 'Latin' secretary to Cromwell.

certain germs from which a genuinely Italian literature might, in course of time, have been, and actually was, to some extent, developed: such were, for instance, sepulchral inscriptions, family records, and so forth; ritual hymns, couched in the native 'Saturnian' metre, the so-called 'Fescennine verses' sung at harvest-homes, and the dramatic *săturae* or 'medleys' without any regular plot and containing a good deal of banter and invective. The last-mentioned especially are important as the progenitors—at least in name—of the later literary *satura*, which the Romans always claimed as native to their soil. Although these various elements were by no means unimportant in respect of their influence on the matter and form of the subsequent literature, it is none the less true that their natural growth and operation were seriously and permanently affected by the circumstance that the first Roman authors worthy of the name required a literary model, and that that model was Greek. The history of Roman literature in the first period which we shall define is largely the history of the attempt to naturalize certain Greek literary forms in the Roman tongue: in some cases (e.g. the drama) this attempt represents the height of achievement, in others (e.g. epic poetry), it paves the way for fuller conquests, especially in the matter of technical finish, in a subsequent period.

§ 97. Four Periods of Latin Literature

In the history of Latin literature we may conveniently distinguish four main periods: (i) 240–80 B.C.; (ii) 80–40 B.C.; (iii) 40 B.C.–A.D. 17; (iv) A.D. 17–130. The first of these is sometimes spoken of as the pre-Ciceronian or ante-classical period, the second as the Ciceronian, the third as the Augustan, and the fourth as the Silver Age. The second and third periods together represent the Golden Age of Latin literature.

A. *First Period*, 240–80 B.C.

The development of poetry before prose was characteristic of Roman as of other literatures. The first Roman author was **Livius Andrŏnicus** (*c.* 284–204 B.C.), a Greek who was taken prisoner at the capture of Tarentum (272) and brought to Rome, where he learned Latin and secured the citizenship through the patronage of M. Livius Sălīnātor. Livius wrote both tragedies and comedies, which were borrowed or translated from the Greek, and also a translation of the *Odyssey* in the Saturnian metre,[1] which was long used as a school-book.

Livius' successor, **Cn. Naevius** (d. *c.* 200 B.C.), was probably a Campanian by birth and served in the First Punic War. Naevius adapted both tragedies and comedies, but especially the latter, from the Greek, and composed a poem, in Saturnian verse, on the First Punic War, which was used by both Ennius and Virgil.

A greater figure than either Livius or Naevius, however, was **Q. Ennius** (239–169 B.C.), a native of Rudiae, in Calabria, who being brought to Rome in 204 enjoyed the friendship of some of the greatest Romans of his time, notably Scipio Africanus the Elder. Ennius gave tragedy a fresh impulse, and also wrote *Saturae*; but his great achievement, which caused him to be regarded as the father of Roman literature, was his epic poem, in eighteen books, the *Annāles*, in which he traced the story of Rome from Aeneas down to his own times. Of this work only fragments are extant, but these, coupled with the universal testimony of antiquity, are sufficient to mark out Ennius as the greatest creative force in Latin literature before the age of Cicero. The dactylic hexameter which Ennius employed in his poem replaced the Saturnian for good as the medium for epic poetry; and though in Ennius' hands it was little better than a rude experiment, the *Annales* remained, in form as in spirit, the great epic of Rome till it was superseded by the *Aeneid*.

In this period of literary experiment, one department of literature—Comedy—was destined to find its greatest exponent in **Titus Maccius Plautus,** a native of Umbria (254–184 B.C.), twenty of whose comedies have survived to us. The plays of Plautus were very popular in his own day, and

§ 97.   [1] The rhythm of the Saturnian verse resembles that of the nursery rhyme, 'The queen was in the parlour, eating bread and honey.'

continued to be read and admired by educated Romans down to the latest times. Plautus found his models in the New Comedy of Athens, as represented especially by Menander, and owed his popularity less to any brilliant manipulation of the plot of his original than to wealth of fun, broad humour, and vivacity of dialogue. The merit of Plautus' work, although something must be conceded to the chance which has preserved for us such a large amount of it while others are represented by fragments or not at all, may be gauged to some extent by the influence he has exercised on modern comedy and by the fact that several of his plays have been directly imitated by modern poets.

Rather different in character, but coupled with Plautus as the other great exponent of Roman Comedy who can be judged by extant remains, was **P. Terentius Āfer** (185–159 B.C.), usually known as **Terence,** a native of Carthage, who was brought to Rome, and there educated and manumitted by Terentius Lūcānus, a senator. At Rome Terence enjoyed the intimate friendship of a select literary circle, the chief members of which were Gaius Laelius and Scipio Africanus the Younger, who were even reputed to have assisted him in his literary productions. Terence is represented by six comedies in all, which were universally allowed the qualities of propriety of sentiment and studious elegance of diction, while lacking in dramatic power and in the boisterous spirits of Plautus. His hard and sometimes unsuccessful efforts to secure a hearing for his plays are to be explained, to a large extent, by the fact that these were really addressed more to his literary patrons than to the public at large.

Besides Plautus and Terence, we have the names, in Comedy, of **Caecilius Stātius**, a native of Mediolānum (*Milan*) and the immediate predecessor of Terence, and of **Lucius Afrānius** (fl. *c*. 120 B.C.), who wrote *comoediae togatae* depicting Roman scenes and manners; and, in Tragedy, of **M. Pācŭvius**, sister's son to Ennius, who is placed by Cicero at the head of Roman Tragedy, and of **L. Accius,** a younger contemporary, both of whom were authors of tragedies taken from the Greek and also of some dealing with Roman subjects and known as *Praetextae*.

In the department of the native *satura*, an outstanding figure and the first to invest it with definite literary shape was **Gaius Lūcīlius** (180–102 B.C.), whose *Miscellanies*, if loose and careless in texture, were certainly characterized by an outspokenness and boldness of invective which did not hesitate to assail

SCENE FROM A TRAGEDY
Terra-cotta grave monument

the most distinguished personalities of the day. In another aspect the *Miscellanies* appear to have been something in the nature of an autobiography. Only fragments remain of Lucilius' work, which, had it been preserved, would have been of surpassing interest.

Side by side with poetry, which constitutes the main interest of this period, we find a growing interest in oratory on its

practical side, though as yet it is barely represented by any rhetorical treatise; history is represented by a series of chroniclers,
who, while hardly worthy of the title of historians, did useful
work in gathering the materials of history. In this connexion
may be mentioned the *Ŏrīgines* of **Cato the Censor** (234–
149 B.C.), a work on ancient Roman and Italian history, which
no doubt bore the impress of the rugged character of its author,
if we may judge by another treatise of Cato's—his *De Agri
Cultūra*—which has been preserved to us, and which is of special
interest as the earliest extant monument of Roman prose literature.

Summing up, we may characterize the first period as a time
of experiment in the adaptation of Greek models to the needs
of the Latin language: dramatic literature (both tragic and
comic) reaches its high-water mark: the *satura* receives a definite
literary setting in the hands of Lucilius, as does the epic in the
hands of Ennius: prose is feeling its way towards a satisfying
artistic shape.

B. *Second Period,* 80–40 B.C.

In the second period, usually known as the Ciceronian after
its most brilliant representative, prose reaches its highest and
purest excellence in the hands of **Cicero** (oratory) and **Caesar**
and **Sallust** (history). With regard to the oratorical part of
Cicero's activity, it should be remembered that his speeches
were intended quite as much for the reading public, which now
existed, as for the juries to whom they were immediately
addressed: some of his extant speeches, indeed, were never
delivered at all, but published as pamphlets which would be
read as specimens of artistic composition as well as for their
political interest.

Marcus Tullius Cicero (106–43 B.C.), born at Arpīnum,
the birthplace of Marius, and educated at Rome, appeared as
a pleader at the age of twenty-five, rose through the various
grades of public office to the consulship (63), when he sup-
pressed the famous conspiracy of Catiline, and was murdered by
Antony's soldiers in the proscriptions of 43. As a man of letters,

Cicero falls to be considered under the heads of (1) orator, (2) writer on oratory, (3) philosopher, (4) letter-writer.

(1) It was on his oratory that Cicero himself would have based his chief claim to fame. We have now some sixty of his speeches, covering roughly forty years of his life (81–43). Of the various types of oratory which they represent, the forensic was perhaps best suited to his peculiar gifts, among which may be reckoned a power of graphic description, brilliant wit, moving pathos, combined with a hitherto unexampled wealth of phrase and richness of diction. As a pleader, he was happiest in defence, and, when there were others 'with him' in a case, usually reserved himself for a final powerful appeal to the jury.

Notable *groups* of speeches, representing, on the whole, his early, mid, and late career, respectively, are those *Against Verres*, the rapacious governor of Sicily (six—70); *Against Catiline* (four —63); and the fourteen *Philippics* against Antony (44–43), of which the second was famous.

(2) No one was better entitled than Cicero, by education and practical experience, to pronounce on the training and qualifications of an orator, which he discusses in his *De Oratore*, a treatise in three books, in dialogue form, in which the chief speakers are the noted rival orators, L. Crassus and M. Antonius. The *Brutus* or *De Claris Oratoribus* is a survey of the history of Roman eloquence.

(3) In the sphere of philosophy, in which the bulk of his large output (*De Re Publica*, *De Lēgibus*, *De Fīnibus*, *Acadēmica*, *Tusŭclānae Dispŭtationes*, *De Nātūra Deorum*, *De Dīvīnatione*, *De Officiis*, and the two charming essays *De Senectute*, 'On Old Age', and *De Amicitia*, 'On Friendship') belongs to the last two years of his life, Cicero did not claim to be original: his great service was to make available for his countrymen the results of Greek thought in their own language, and, incidentally, to perfect a literary style which has exerted an important influence on the prose style of modern Western Europe.

(4) There are extant nearly eight hundred letters addressed by Cicero to various correspondents, and about a hundred addressed to Cicero by others. These fall into four collections:

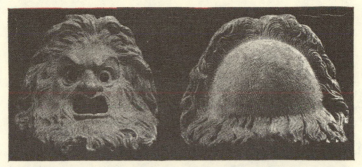

A SATIRIC MASK. Palazzo dei Conservatori, Rome

COMIC ACTORS. From a Vatican MS. of Terence (ninth century). The Latin begins at *Adelphoe*, 1. 889 where old Demea assumes an indulgent and genial manner

(*a*) *Ad Atticum* (a banker and Cicero's most intimate friend: sixteen books, 68–43); (*b*) *Ad Quintum Fratrem*; (*c*) *Ad Brutum*; (*d*) *Ad Familiares* ('To several of his friends': sixteen books, 62–43).

The charm of these letters depends largely on the fact that they were not intended for publication, and so are marked by extreme frankness and self-revelation. Colloquial in style and abounding with Greek expressions and quotations, they form a sort of mirror of Cicero's personal interests and activities and of the internal politics of contemporary Rome.

Gaius Iulius Caesar [100–44 B.C.: consul, 59; defeated Pompey at Pharsalus, 48; assassinated by Brutus, Cassius, &c., 44] was the author of seven books of *Commentarii* ('Notes') on his campaigns in Gaul, Germany, and Britain (*De Bello Gallico*) during the years 58–52 B.C., and of three books on the Civil War (*De Bello Cīvīli*) with Pompey, to both of which additions were made by other hands. Apart from their objective interest, these works have always been highly rated for their qualities of style—lucidity, self-restraint, and purity of language—which have made Caesar favourite reading in the schools and a model for Latin prose.

Gaius Sallustius Crispus (86–35 B.C.) is known to us mainly as the author of the two historical monographs—on the conspiracy of Catiline (*Bellum Catilinae*) and on the war with Jugurtha (*Bellum Iugurthīnum*). As a historian, Sallust was the first who aimed at treating a given episode or period as an artistic unity, as opposed to the annalistic arrangement which had been the rule before his time, and at tracing the motives of actions. His style, which he modelled on that of the Greek historian Thucydides, is brief, terse, and epigrammatic, and anticipates, in many respects, that of Tacitus.

The period under review was also marked by the production of technical and scientific treatises, in which connexion there falls to be mentioned the name of **M. Terentius Varro** (116–27 B.C.), the learned and voluminous antiquarian, who was active at the age of eighty and whose immense learning ranged over almost every field of human knowledge. The list of prose writers may be closed with the name of **Cornelius Něpos**

(99–24 B.C.), author of a work *De Viris Illustribus*, consisting of parallel lives of Roman and foreign celebrities, arranged in sixteen books; but neither he nor Varro can claim a place by the side of the first three as a master of prose style.

While prose had thus reached a high level of development, poetry, which seemed for the time to have exhausted itself and to be awaiting some fresh impulse, is represented by two isolated names, but these of the first importance, **Titus Lucrētius Cārus** and **Gaius Valerius Catullus**.

Lucretius (*c.* 94–55 B.C.), of whose life we have very scanty knowledge, expounded the philosophical system of Epicurus in a remarkable poem in six books, entitled *De Rerum Natura*, with the avowed object of delivering mankind from superstitious terrors and the fear of death. The subject selected by Lucretius for his purpose inevitably gives rise to passages of severely technical exposition; but even these are successfully surmounted by his poetic genius which overcomes the most unpromising materials. The poet's powers of observation, his wonderfully fresh and penetrating eye for nature, the beauty of his digressions when for a moment he takes leave of abstruse speculation, and the tremendous earnestness which pervades the whole work, combine to make the *De Rerum Natura* the most remarkable didactic poem of all time. Virgil, himself a sympathetic student of nature, among subsequent poets bears abundant traces of the influence of Lucretius.

Catullus (*c.* 84–54 B.C.), a native of Verona, in North Italy, is known for all time as the singer of Lesbia—identified with Clodia, sister of the notorious P. Clodius, the enemy of Cicero —his early passion for whom forms the central theme of (i) the lyric pieces, mainly in the hendecasyllabic (eleven-syllable) metre, to which he owes his fame. In addition to these, we have (ii) six longer poems, in the heroic, elegiac, and other metres, including the *Marriage of Pēleus and Thĕtis*, the two *Epithălāmia* (marriage hymns), and the *Atys* or *Attis*, representing his most pretentious work; and (iii) a number of epigrams, on various subjects, all in the elegiac metre.

Catullus' striking qualities as a lyric poet may be said to be the absolute frankness and spontaneity with which he gives expression to the emotion of the moment—whether it be love or hate—together with a seemingly unstudied simplicity of language which makes a direct appeal to the reader.

C. *Third Period: The Augustan Age*, 40 B.C.–A.D. 17

The establishment of the empire under Augustus, an event of profound importance for the Roman world, was also important as determining the general character of the literature which was to lend a lustre to the early imperial period. The suppression of independent political thought and action tended to starve oratory and contemporary history—the two great forms of prose literature—by cutting off the streams which had fed them under the republic, while it gave a corresponding impulse to poetry, which was less dependent on a strenuous and first-hand participation in the political events of the day as a condition of vigorous life. The keynote of this poetry was the enthusiasm evoked by the restoration of peace to the Roman world under the beneficent rule of Augustus, the hoped-for rehabilitation of all that had made Rome great in the past, and the emperor-worship of which Augustus himself was the object. Augustus, on his part, dexterously enlisted the services of the poets in support of the new political and moral régime which he was setting out to establish, and in this he had the able support of his minister *Maecēnas*, who was a great patron of letters. We thus find the great poets of the Augustan age marshalled, to some extent, in a distinct coterie under the conscious patronage of the court, in whose shade they write and to whose ideas they give voice. But further, the blessings of peace and prosperity gave poetry a more personal and introspective turn, which found expression in the *Elegy*, the recognized vehicle of the poetry of the pleasures and interests of private life.

With regard to prose, while the writing of contemporary history was less likely to be informed by the experience of active political life, the greater leisure which the empire made possible rendered the time eminently suitable for the composition of a great national history which should gather up the results of previous labours in the same field and weave them into a sympathetic and imaginative whole— a work which was admirably accomplished by Livy.

The general principles enunciated above are illustrated in the work of the great names of the Augustan age—**Virgil** and **Horace**; the elegists **Tibullus, Propertius,** and **Ovid**; and in the historian **Livy.**

Publius Vergilius Măro (70–19 B.C.) was born near Mantua, in North Italy, but spent his life mainly in the south, in Campania and at Rome. He was a prominent member of the literary circle of Maecenas, who introduced him to Augustus, and was intimate with Horace. He died at Brundisium on his return from a visit to Greece (19 B.C.), and was buried at Naples, where his tomb was shown.

The chief works of Virgil are (i) the *Bucolics* or *Eclogues* (42–37), consisting of ten pieces modelled more or less closely on the pastoral poetry of the Greek poet Theocritus; (ii) the *Georgics* (36–29), a didactic poem on agriculture, in four books, which ranks, in point of literary execution, as the most finished of Virgil's works; and (iii) the *Aeneid*, an epic poem in twelve books, which occupied roughly the last ten years of the poet's life and had not received the finishing touches at his death.

The *Aeneid*, so called from the Trojan prince Aeneas, whose adventures on his voyagings from Troy and subsequent fortunes in Italy, up to the death of his rival Turnus, form the historical setting of the poem, may be said to have for its true subject the glories of Rome and her destinies under Augustus as her second founder. From its publication the *Aeneid* at once took its place as the great national epic of Rome and still stands, by common consent, as one of the great epics of the world. Among its distinctive excellences may be mentioned its wealth of associations—historical, mythological, antiquarian—deep pathos, profound religious feeling, and a richness and variety of rhythm, especially in the later books, which shows the hexameter at the highest pitch of technical perfection.

Quintus Horātius Flaccus (65–8 B.C.), born at Venusia

and educated at Rome and later at Athens, fought in Brutus' army at Philippi (42), and after his return to Rome, where his fortunes were for some time at a low ebb, was introduced by Virgil to Maecenas and enjoyed the friendship of Augustus. From Maecenas he received an estate in the Sabine country, for which he conceived a great affection, and where he spent much of his time. He died in 8 B.C., a few months after his patron.

Horace's works comprise (a) two books of *Satires*, called by himself *Sermones* or 'talks', and a book of *Epodes*, published 35–30 B.C.; (b) the *Odes* (*Carmina*) in four books, of which the first three were published together, 23 B.C., and the fourth ten years later; (c) the *Epistulae*, to various friends, in two books, of which the first belongs to 20 B.C. and the second to about 13 B.C. The *Epistula ad Pisones* or *Ars Poetica* was probably written after the *Carmen Saeculare*, composed for the *Ludi Saeculares* of 17 B.C.

The *Satires* are written, like the *Epistles*, in a loose hexameter verse, and deal with social and literary topics, or human foibles, in a tone of good-natured banter which distinguishes Horace as a satirist alike from his predecessor Lucilius and his successor Juvenal. The *Epistles* are largely similar in content, but in a more careful style, and contain many precepts of shrewd worldly wisdom which have won their way to proverbs. The *Art of Poetry* is an essay in literary criticism, dealing especially with the rules of the drama.

It is on the *Odes*, however, that Horace's poetical fame most securely rests. These are founded closely on Greek lyrics, chiefly those of Sappho and Alcaeus, and their themes range from the lighter ones of love and wine to graver topics of moral or political interest.

As a love-poet, Horace is passionless, compared with Catullus, and his philosophy of life does not transcend the commonplace; but the brilliantly finished form in which that philosophy finds expression, and the ease with which many a perfectly turned sentiment can be detached from its context, have combined to make Horace the most quoted of the classical poets and have found for him translators and adaptors in every civilized language.

Albius Tibullus was most probably a native of the district of Pedum, in Latium, and his birth falls somewhere in the decade 58–48 B.C. He belonged to the literary coterie of Messalla Corvinus, to whom he was much attached and whom he followed in his campaigns. He died apparently the same year as Virgil (19 B.C.).

Four books of elegiac poems are current under the name of Tibullus, of which only the first two are certainly genuine, the chief themes being his mistresses Delia (whose real name was Plania) and Nemesis, respectively. Apart from the subjects furnished by his love and the praise of his patron, Tibullus excels in portraying the quiet joys of country life in smooth and melodious verse coupled with purity of diction. Without being a poet of great genius, he is a poet who pleases; and he was highly thought of both by Horace and by Quintilian.

Sextus Propertius (born *c.* 50; died between 16 B.C. and A.D. 2) was born at Asisium (*Assisi*) in Umbria. Brought to Rome by his mother after his father's death, he appears to have studied law for a short time, but abandoned this in favour of poetry. In 29 or 28 began his acquaintance with the Cynthia of his poems, who occupies much the same place in relation to Propertius' life and poetry as Lesbia does to Catullus'. Propertius belonged to the literary circle of Maecenas: he expresses warm admiration of Virgil and was intimate with Ovid.

The work of Propertius comprises four books of *Elegies* (the division into five lacks authority): the first two are almost entirely devoted to the subject of Cynthia and reflect the lover's varying moods; in the third and fourth room is found for other topics of mythological or national interest. As a poet, Propertius claims kin with the Alexandrian school in his wealth of mythological allusion and his familiarity with the whole range of Greek poetry. With a certain morbid introspection he combines a note of strong patriotism. In his hands the elegiac metre, in his earlier manner, exhibits a power and flexibility unmatched elsewhere in Latin poetry: in his later, it is more rigid, but there is no loss of technical mastery or poetic power.

Publius Ovidius Nāso (43 B.C.–A.D. 18) belonged to a

well-to-do family of Sulmo, in the country of the Paeligni. Carefully educated at Rome, he was intended for the bar, but the attractions of poetry proved irresistible; and Ovid, abandoning the idea of a public career, lived a congenial life as the fashionable poet of the capital till he had passed his fiftieth year, when he was suddenly required, by an edict of Augustus, to withdraw to Tomis, a place on the Black Sea, not far from the mouth of the Danube. The cause of his banishment is obscure, but the decree was not revoked, and he died at Tomis, A.D. 18.

Ovid's works fall easily into three groups: (1) love poetry, including the *Amores*, elegies addressed to a (probably fictitious) mistress, Corinna; the *Hērōïdes*, a series of letters addressed by heroines of antiquity to their lovers; and the *Ars Amātōria*, a poem on love-intrigue; (2) mythological poetry, represented by the *Metamorphōses* or *Transformations* of human beings, after some profound crisis in their fortunes, into animals, trees, etc. (fifteen books), and the *Fasti*, a poetical calendar of the Roman year (six books); (3) poems of his exile, comprising the five books of *Tristia*, and the four books of *Epistulae ex Ponto*, addressed to Augustus, his wife, or to friends at Rome, and dealing generally with the miseries of his exile and the causes of his punishment. All the works mentioned, with the exception of the *Metamorphoses*, which is in a light hexameter, are in the elegiac metre.

Ovid's chief qualities are a remarkable talent for storytelling, which he displays to the full in the *Metamorphoses*, and a wonderful facility in versification. As employed by him, the elegiac couplet, within the somewhat rigid limits which he imposed upon it (e.g. the rule that a dissyllabic word must end the pentameter), reaches its highest perfection; and his influence and popularity in subsequent ages have perhaps been out of proportion to his merit.

Titus Livius was born at Patavium (*Padua*) in the year 59 B.C. Little is known of his life. He probably settled at Rome about the age of thirty, with a view to the preparation of his History, and there he became intimate with Augustus. He appears to have returned later to his native town, where he died at the age of 76, A.D. 17, with his fame already established.

Livy's great work, the title of which seems to have been *Ab urbe condita libri*, was probably planned to consist of 150 books, ending with the death of Augustus (A.D. 14): he actually completed 142, ending with the death of Drusus (stepson of Augustus and brother of Tiberius—9 B.C.). The number of books now extant is 35, viz. i–x, which carry the history down to 293 B.C., and xxi–xlv (of which xli and xliii are incomplete), covering the period 218–167 B.C. The division into books is due to Livy himself: the division into decades (sets of ten books) is a late conventional arrangement.

As a historian, Livy can hardly be said to satisfy modern standards: he adopts an easy-going attitude towards his authorities and is culpably negligent in his failure to consult at first hand ancient monuments and documents which must have been easily accessible. It is as an artist in prose that Livy is admittedly great: he is the most eloquent of historians. He has a keenly patriotic enthusiasm, a vivid imagination, and a rich and varied vocabulary, occasionally tinged with a poetic colouring which looks forward from the golden to the silver age of Latin prose.

D. Fourth Period: The Silver Age, A.D. 17–c. 130

The century following the death of Augustus is on the whole a period of decay, but within it there are temporary revivals and some outstanding names, especially towards its close. The reigns of Tiberius (14–37) and Claudius (41–54) were not marked by any important additions to literature, but a fresh impulse was given by the accession of Nero, who himself dabbled in letters. The two most interesting names of the Neronian age (54–68) are those of the uncle and nephew, **L. Annaeus Seneca** (*c.* 4 B.C.–A.D. 65) and **M. Annaeus Lūcānus** (39–65), both representatives of a Spanish family; for the provinces were now beginning to reinforce the apparently outworn resources of Italy proper. **Seneca,** in the course of his chequered career as a courtier, wrote voluminously on moral and kindred topics, mainly from the point of view of the Stoic philosophy, in a style characterized by too much glitter and too continual a straining after epigrammatic point to carry with it a complete conviction of sincerity. He also composed a number of tragedies which had a great influence on the English drama of the sixteenth century. **Lucan,** who died young, involved, like his uncle, in a conspiracy against Nero, was the author of the *Pharsālia*, a poem on the civil war between Caesar and Pompey, in which rhetorical declamation is carried to an extravagant pitch, though the poem has a rugged force and vigour of its own and abounds in striking passages which quotation has made familiar. To the names of Seneca and Lucan may be added those of another disciple of the Stoic school, the satirist **Persius** (34–62), and **Petronius Arbiter**, author of a satirical prose novel, of which Trimalchio's Dinner Party (*Cena Trimalchionis*) is a large fragment surviving almost complete, a masterpiece of vivid, ribald narrative and dialogue.

Under the Flavian emperors (Vespasian, Titus, Domitian, 69–96) the rhetorical extravagance of the age of Nero gave place to a more sober tone. The authors calling for chief remark are the poets **Statius** and **Martial**, and, among prose writers, **Pliny the Elder** and **Quintilian**.

P. Papinius Stātius (*c.* 45–96) wrote epic poems (*Thēbăis, Achillēis*) displaying careful technical execution rather than originality of genius, more interesting than which are his five books of *Silvae*, a collection of occasional poems on various subjects. The epigrams of **Marcus Valerius Martialis** (*c.* 40–104), a Spaniard by birth, are invaluable as a mirror of his age and of the daily life of Rome as it was in his time.

C. Plinius Secundus (23–79) was the compiler of the famous *Natural History* (*Nātūrālis Histŏria*), and otherwise a man of immense literary activity. He perished in the eruption of Vesuvius, A.D. 79. **M. Fabius Quintilianus** (35–*c.* 100), another Spaniard, and the first endowed professor of rhetoric at Rome, was the author of the famous *Institūtio Ōrātōria*, which remained the standard treatise on the theory and practice of Latin oratory, and contains much just and sound criticism of classical writers.

The third and closing portion of the Silver Age—that

represented by the reigns of Nerva and Trajan (96–117)—furnishes the two great figures of Tacitus and Juvenal.

Cornelius Tacitus (*c.* 55–*c.* 120) was the author of *Historiae* from the beginning of A.D. 69 to the death of Domitian (96), and of *Annales*, extending from the death of Augustus probably to the accession of Galba (A.D. 68); but there are now considerable gaps in both works. In addition to these, there are the *Agricola*, a biography of his father-in-law, and the *Germania*, a treatise on the geography and ethnology of Germany, together with his earliest work of all, the *Dialogue on Orators*. As a historian, Tacitus is inspired with a burning sense of indignation against what he considers the injustice of the empire, which he accepts as a necessary evil; and if he cannot be said to distort his facts, he succeeds in investing them with a malignant light. His style in its mature shape is unique in Latin literature, being distinguished by variety, brevity, and poetic complexion, in which last aspect it contains numerous reminiscences of Virgil. Many epigrammatic phrases which have passed into proverbs may be detached from his writings.

Decimus Iunius Iuvenalis (*c.* 67–*c.* 130) found scope for his 'indignation' in the recognized channel of satire, which in his hands is characterized by vigour of expression and a power of vivid description. There is an obvious proneness to exaggeration: Juvenal strikes us as reserving the vials of his wrath for the most venial offences: Nero the matricide is a respectable figure beside Nero the harpist; but the undoubted power of the declamation does much to condone the distorted view of the satirist. Perhaps the most famous of the sixteen satires are the third, which gives a picture of life at Rome, and the tenth, well known in its modern dress as Johnson's 'Vanity of Human Wishes'.

It is pleasing to turn from the sombre picture of Tacitus and Juvenal to the brighter atmosphere of the *Letters* of **Pliny the Younger**, which do something to correct our impression of the depravity of Roman life and morals in the early Empire.

Gaius Plinius Secundus, or **Pliny the Younger**, as he is usually called to distinguish him from his uncle (author of the

Natural History), was born at Novum Comum, in North Italy,
A.D. 61 or 62, and later studied rhetoric under the best teachers
at Rome. He was in attendance on his uncle (who adopted
him in his will) in August A.D. 79, when the famous eruption of
Vesuvius took place in which the latter lost his life. At Rome
Pliny made some mark at the bar and rose rapidly in the public
service, becoming consul in A.D. 100, an honour for which he
thanked Trajan in his *Pănēgў̄ricus*. Some years later he was
appointed by Trajan governor of the province of Pontus and
Bithynia, where he probably died, before A.D. 114.

Pliny's *Letters*, of which we have nine books, followed by his
correspondence with Trajan, were designed to present us with
a picture of the various interests and occupations of a cultivated
Roman gentleman of the time, and convey an entirely favourable impression of the personality of the writer himself. In the
matter of style, Pliny sought to imitate Cicero, but his letters
differ from Cicero's in that they were consciously written for
publication. Two of the best known (sixth book) are those in
which he describes the eruption of Vesuvius to his friend
Tacitus, the historian, while the most famous of those to Trajan
is that in which he asks the emperor's advice regarding the
treatment of the Christians in his province.

With the death of Juvenal, Roman literature as a living force
may be said to close; in the next two centuries there was
a rapid decline in both poetry and prose, though the latter
acquired something like a new lease of life in the hands of the
early Christian apologists. We may extend our survey slightly
so as to include **C. Suetonius Tranquillus** (*c.* 69–*c.* 140), who
is represented now by his 'Lives of the Caesars' (*De Vita
Caesarum*), written in a simple and direct style and containing
great wealth of anecdote.

§ 98. Writing and Writing Materials

The materials used for writing purposes were (i) wooden
tablets covered with wax (*cōdex, cōdĭcillus*), (ii) *păpȳrus*, (iii) parchment (*membrāna pergămēna*). *Papyrus* (whence our *paper*—also
called *charta*) was prepared from the inner tissue of the

papyrus reed and exported from Egypt; *parchment*, a preparation of sheep-skin, so called from the city of Pergamum, where
it is said to have been first used, was a thicker and more durable
and also cheaper material, which after being long considered
inferior to *papyrus* finally ousted it for the purposes of book-
making. Wax-covered tablets were specially employed for brief
notes, the writing being performed by means of a sharp-
pointed instrument (*stĭlus*). Erasures were effected or a fresh
surface prepared by rubbing over the wax with the thick upper
end of the *stilus*—hence the expression *stilum vertere* = 'to erase
what has been written'. Writing on papyrus or parchment,
however, was executed by means of a reed-pen (*călămus*),
dipped in ink (*atrāmentum*) made of lamp-black and gum.

§ 99. Construction of a Book

The word *lĭber* (lit. 'bark') preserves the memory of a time
when the bark of trees was used for writing upon; but papyrus
was the material in general use for literary compositions, and
only began to give way to parchment in the fourth century A.D.
In form, an ordinary Roman 'book' did not resemble a modern
one, but was literally what the name *vŏlūmen* or *volume* implies—
a roll. Strips of papyrus were gummed together into sheets,
which were each inscribed with a column of writing (*păgĭna*),
running from left to right: the sheets were then pasted together
at the sides in proper order. When a sufficient number of sheets
had been so dealt with, a stick, often with ornamented ends
(*umbĭlĭcus*), was attached to the last sheet,[1] and round this the
whole was rolled into a *volumen*. The ends of the cylinder (*frontes*)
were then smoothed off with pumice-stone (*pūmex*) and often
coloured black. A piece of parchment (*tĭtŭlus, index*) bearing the
title of the work was attached to the upper end of the roll,
which was sometimes enclosed in a parchment case, with the
index, however, exposed.

In reading, the roll was held in the right hand and unwound

---

§ 99.   [1] According to another view the *umbilicus* was free, and could be
inserted or withdrawn at pleasure.

with the left: with the left also the reader rolled up the portion which he had already perused (*evolvere, explicare*).

Parchment, owing to its greater thickness and toughness, had the advantage over papyrus that it could be written on on both sides, and this property no doubt led to parchment books being made up in the modern form, that is, in separate leaves bound together at the back. Such a book was technically known as a *cōdex*, and came into general use in the fourth century A.D. It was in use earlier among the Christian communities of Egypt, who perhaps invented it.

§ 100. Publication: Booksellers

A literary work was 'published' in the first instance usually by means of a public recitation. The author then took his work to a publisher who prepared an 'edition' by a staff of copyists, who either wrote from dictation or had the author's copy distributed in parts among them. What arrangements, if any, were come to between author and publisher in the way of profits, we do not know. When the edition was prepared, the book was advertised for sale on the bookseller's door-posts or on the pillars of the portico under which the books were displayed. The book trade at Rome was well established in the time of Cicero: the brothers Sosii were a well-known firm in the time of Horace, as Tryphon was in the time of Quintilian and Martial. Books were apparently sold at a reasonable figure within the reach of persons of humble means, though the price no doubt varied according to the 'get up' of the volume. Public libraries, moreover, were numerous, no fewer that twenty-six of these being said to have existed in Rome at the beginning of the fourth century A.D.

§ 101. How the Classical Authors have been Preserved

Copies of the works of the more notable Roman authors, multiplied by copyists in the way described, not without the making of a good many mistakes in the process, may be presumed to have been fairly numerous in the early centuries of

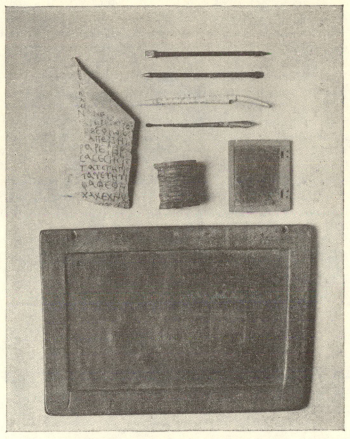

ROMAN WRITING MATERIALS. *Stili* (writing implements), an ink-pot,
writing-tablets, and a pupil's exercise

Photograph British Museum

the Christian era. In the Middle Ages the work of copying manuscripts became part of the daily routine in the monasteries as an antidote to unholy thoughts, the Benedictine monks being especially noteworthy in this connexion. When the revival of learning came in the fourteenth century, largely through the influence of the Italian masters of style—Dante, Petrarch, and Boccaccio—an enthusiasm was aroused for the recovery of the literary masters of a bygone age. Eager scholars in different countries of Europe—Italy, England, France, Switzerland—ransacked the monasteries and brought their hidden treasures to light, with the result that a large part of the Latin classics was discovered in the course of the century between 1350 and 1450. It will also appear how the great majority of our extant MSS.—copies of an original long since lost—date to the fourteenth and fifteenth centuries. The invention of printing, about the middle of the fifteenth century, secured the preservation and also the diffusion of the classics. From that date the classics have formed a regular branch of study in the universities of Western Europe, and have been expounded and commented upon by a succession of able scholars in many countries.